my India my Canada

finding my place
between two cultures

Nityanand Sharma

◆ FriesenPress

Suite 300 - 990 Fort St
Victoria, BC, V8V 3K2
Canada

www.friesenpress.com

ISBN
978-1-5255-0653-6 (Hardcover)
978-1-5255-0654-3 (Paperback)
978-1-5255-0655-0 (eBook)

1. BIOGRAPHY & AUTOBIOGRAPHY, PERSONAL MEMOIRS

Distributed to the trade by The Ingram Book Company

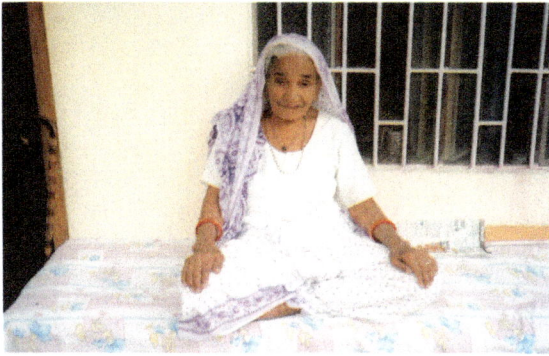

This book is dedicated to my mother, who passed away happily on July 7, 2016 in India at the age of 107. She always wanted to be with us, but was living with the larger family of her other children and grandchildren. She considered traveling abroad to be with us too cumbersome in terms of applying for passport, visa, and medical insurance and because of the long passage in the air. She did not wish to change her lifestyle in a new country that was very different from her own, but she also knew that I was not leaving the country after sponsoring my family to live here in Canada.

I am celebrating the life of my mother, who blessed me and my family from a distance sitting in India while we were half the world away from her.

I am also happy to celebrate the fact that this publication of my autobiography coincides with the celebrations taking place for 150th birthday of Canada.

Table of Contents

Editor's Note

My India, My Canada is a compelling read about an interesting life in memorable surroundings and circumstances. The Author has a real knack for telling a story and including just the right amount of description and detail so that the reader feels like he/she has shared in the events described. Canadians and other readers will be fascinated by reading about the Author's youth in India – for example, his stories about having to take cattle to water when he was only six and worrying about cobras when walking at night. The readers will also be intrigued by the cultural differences (both real and perceived) between his new country and country of birth. For instance, I found the list of questions that Canadians asked him about India quite telling of the fact that we have many misconceptions about life in other countries. I also enjoyed rediscovering our country through his eyes as a newcomer. Likewise, his sense of humor helps reveal his personality and make the experience of reading his story more personal and engaging. Many of his stories made me laugh out loud, such as the one about him giving the irate driver two fingers back when he showed him his one finger.

His poetry, notes about English expressions from when he first moved here, and beautiful pictures are also wonderful additions that make his book vibrant, unique, and highly readable.

Nityanand's story is a well-written manuscript. I really enjoyed reading the story of his life, and I believe others will as well. I would like to congratulate him on capturing his interesting life so well on paper and for having the openness to share it with others.

Friesen Press Editor

Introduction

On July 4, 1940, I was born in the village of Lotwara in Rajasthan, India. My father, Laxmi Narayan, and my mother, Bhauti Devi Sharma, were from the Brahmin caste. My family all say I was a bundle of joy! After my birth, my parents had three more sons and one daughter. My father was the eldest son of a prominent landowner and a money lender, which in a small village made us "prominent". I was seen as a precious child of this family due to being the first-born son.

My grandfather and great grandfather arranged an elaborate celebration when I was born, which included the sounding of drums; dancing and singing inside and outside our home; distributing sweets and gifts to village members; inviting relatives, friends, and neighbors for poetry recitation sessions; and a special gathering of friends and family members with an ongoing feast. Special packages for various types of celebrations kept coming as I was growing up, including when I was introduced to solid food after four months; when I uttered my first word; when I learned to crawl; when I took my first steps; when I had my first haircut; and when I started my first day of school, as part of our cultural and family traditions.

At the age of three, my grandfather passed my handheld crib under the Hindu God Lord Krishna's altar during a divine procession on Krishna Janmasthmi day (Divine Krishna's birthday) in front of hundreds of people just to ensure that my life would be blessed by divine Krishna and that I would have a happy and prosperous life. I was named Nityanand, which means "every day pleasure".

Introduction

On July 4, 2016, I celebrated my 76th birthday! I feel very blessed to be still enjoying everyday pleasures and watching my children and grandchildren grow. This book is about my stories in life so far and all the beauty I have witnessed in this world.

I feel that I should share my story with Canadians and other immigrants about the passion one feels to move to another country and how it feels to leave his or her own Motherland.

I had a good academic background from India when I arrived in Canada. I had completed a Bachelor of Commerce Degree specializing in Commercial Law, as well as a Masters of Economics specializing in Public Administration and International Banking. I also worked as an Accounts Officer in a private company. I very quickly developed some essential transferable work skills in effectively supervising employees; efficiently organizing, implementing, and initiating programs; and working through organizational politics.

I learnt that one should use the technique of *Saam* (counseling), *Daam* (monetary benefits), *Danda* (discipline of some sort), and *Bhaed* (finding out internal operational strategies) in supervising employees.

These techniques are widely used in most of the successful and profitable organizations back home. I found the techniques very useful as a springboard to implement with adaptations in my surroundings. But this was not enough to work in the New World. I learnt many new operational techniques over and above my own. This kind of background helped me to achieve administrative and supervisory positions in the capacity of principal and education superintendent until I retired. My successful career lasted 31 years due to my training and the practical application of ideas in the jobs I held in Canada.

I tried to learn as much as possible to stay afloat and move ahead. I also received tremendous support from others during my professional life. I tried to work through others by maintaining alliances and by offering my volunteer help wherever possible. Once I knew how to get my job done, I maintained my identity in this part of the world.

One day I was sitting in the living room and pondering on world problems. Kamla suddenly nudged me and said that I think too much about both world and family problems. She also told me that writing my autobiography may or may not do any good, since people are too busy to read a layman's story.

I told Kamla that people would read it as long as it was interesting and genuine and that I wanted to include some themes based on my experience that would provide some food for thought for others. Kamla understood that I was determined to write something useful for everybody but mainly to get my own story down on paper. I hope people will read my autobiography simply because there is something familiar and good for everyone in my story with the pictures.

My story may relate to most immigrants that come to this country. Canadians will find my story interesting, as I have written my experiences with Indian as well as Canadian culture. I have also inserted many great pictures that I took during my travel in Canada and in India to visually complement my story.

My grandfather told me that before you start new work for yourself, your family, and society, we must offer salutation to every being possible for blessings. This makes your job easy and free from all types of hurdles. I must do the same.

Being born in a Hindu family, first of all I must salute the elephant headed Divine deity Ganesha. He is known to remove all obstacles. Then I bow to the goddess of learning who inspires to simplify words, sentences, poetry, and their meaning and fills sweetness in them.

I bow to almighty God, who wears white garments, whose face is benign, and who shines like the moon. He is God Vishnu, who supports the entire universe, along with his consort Goddess Lakshmi, who bestows success, intelligence, wealth, and worldly enjoyment.

I bow to all people – including the saints – good, bad, evil, friend, foe, who rub our lives in some way to shape our destiny and daily living.

I bow to all living beings because they all have divine elements, and I need everyone's blessings. Now I feel at ease to start writing what I have in mind.

CHAPTER ONE
Childhood in the Village Lotwara

Childhood Ritual

Lotwara was a small village with a population of about 500 people. Today Lotwara is a big town with a population of about 10,000 people. The lives of residents were filled with many rituals within the families. I still remember one event when I was three years old. It was a time for me to have my first haircut ceremony in a famous Hanuman (the Monkey God) temple in our village. My great grandfather sat me up in his lap and the barber applied gooseberry oil in my hair. The ladies were busy singing special songs related to this hair cutting ceremony. The songs said that after my haircut I would have long, black, healthy hair forever, and that I would not be influenced by evil looks from anybody. So, the barber shaved off my hair, and I lost my silky baby hair forever.

Despite this, I did get a bald spot at the age of 54! However, even at the age of seventy-six, I still claim that the majority of my hair is black. Perhaps it is because I received a massage of gooseberry oil in 1943 that I continue to enjoy the benefits of having black hair with some strands of grey.

The hair cut ceremony lasted about six hours in the midst of 200 family members, relatives, friends, and our clan of Brahman family members. My grandfather brought me back home, and after some more evening singing and a ritualistic dinner, we slept until the next morning.

A Tragic Event

At the break of dawn, after this special ceremony, there was a big gathering in our household. There were sounds of family members crying, which drew me near to my grandfather, who told me that my great grandfather was no longer with us.

Family members constructed a casket out of rough wood and jute rope. Then they laid my great grandfather on it wrapped in a white cloth. Four people lifted and carried him on their shoulders towards the bank of the river known as Baanganga in our village. I was walking behind every one asking where my great grandfather was going, but no one was saying much about that. Other family members prepared a funeral pyre with a heap of cut logs. They laid my great grandfather on the pyre. It was my grandfather who lit the fire for his father's cremation under the open sky. My grandfather then poked the skull of my great grandfather while the body was being cremated to ensure that the skull was split open. The skull is the hardest body part to break open and to cremate the brains inside of it.

The attendees all took a bath after the cremation. All family members went home and observed twelve days of prayer sessions. I watched it all. I still remember every scene that took place at that time.

In December 1996, I had to do all that when my father passed away. I had to perform all the rites that I observed in 1943. My son will do the same when I pass away, I think. This is the family tradition.

The rites last for twelve days starting with the prayers, cremation of the body, cultural rituals for the peace of the deceased soul, and a feast followed by crowning the eldest son with a turban. Being the eldest son, I had to first light the fire to the pyre in front of the relatives and friends.

The fire lasts for three days to cool off before you can pick up the remains that are spread into the sacred waters of the nearby Holy Ganges River, which I did after three days.

I also shaved my head at that time as a symbol of respect and sacrifice to the deceased soul.

We then opened the feast and had the turban ceremony. As a mark of respect, a number of relatives offered turbans to put on my head as the eldest son. From that day onward, I would be the head of our family.

Family Routines

My grandfather was the head of our family and observed strict discipline in the family's daily routines. He would wake everyone up at 6:00am every morning. Sleeping late was not allowed in our household. My parents had their jobs cut out for them! At the age of six, I was assigned two jobs to perform, besides going to school.

One of them was to prepare a smoke pipe five to six times a day, as my grandfather would have a number of visitors in the morning and evening, and his pipe would go around like a peace pipe among the visitors. He bought raw tobacco from the farmers and always had it ground and ready for a smoke. He always had a good supply for a month in advance.

My grandfather is smoking a pipe that I prepared for him.

The second job I had to perform was to walk five cows, two buffalo, and four bullocks twice a day to a water pond for their daily drink and bath. I enjoyed the second activity very much, especially at dusk, because a couple of my friends used to join me, and we'd have a lot of fun together sharing the activity.

Elementary Schooling

I attended the school in my village from kindergarten to grade five. In grade five, I was 10 years old, and my teacher appointed me his class monitor. I was his favorite student and a smart student too. As a monitor, I would take the attendance and make sure the mats were evenly spread on the floor for every student to sit on, the chalkboard was clean, the duster was dusted, and the school peon was on time. The most difficult part of my job as a monitor was to administer punishment to students who were misbehaving in my class.

Our teacher had designed three "most effective" methods of punishment. One of them was to squeeze a student's fingers with a pencil wedged in between. If a student hit another classmate, the second was to make the student bend down, bring both arms around through his/her legs, and hold on to his/her ears. The student would stand in a corner bending over sometimes for an hour! If a student was found running around, the third punishment was to slap them on their cheeks. This also happened when a student was found talking with other students while the lesson was going on. I did not mind administering the punishment on the students who disliked me or who I didn't like. But I did feel bad when I had to see it applied to my friends.

The biggest problem for me was that if the teacher found me to be lenient in administering the punishment, the punishment would be administered on me. A few times I was slapped for the sake of saving my friends. I particularly remember that classroom.

My favorite activity after school was to hang around with my two friends in the village. We used to run on a narrow path through the middle of the streets in the village. We used to roll a metal ring on the pathways with a rod through a hook. We also used to play with tops and fly kites several times a day. While rolling, and running with the ring, we used to talk about our school and homes. There was nothing else in the village that motivated us. I lived in the village until I completed my grade six.

CHAPTER TWO
Growing Up in Two Different Towns

My Junior High Schooling in a Residence

I went to another school for my junior high grades. The school was about eight kilometers from my village. I was placed in a boarding house so that I would not have to make the long journey every day. This arrangement allowed me to visit my home every weekend and to pick up my basic necessities for the week.

My mother gave me a steel canister in which to put the basic necessities. Every week, I would collect about two Kilograms of wheat flour; small packages of salt, red chillies, coriander, and ginger; about seven potatoes; three tomatoes; and some sweets and a two hundred fifty grams of brown sugar lumps – jag-grey, made out of sugarcane (known as *Guud* in Hindi) – for desserts. I would carry the canister on my head every week to the hostel and empty one back at home at the end of the week. I would arrange my groceries on a corner shelf along with my pots and pans. I had a kerosene stove to cook my meals. I learnt at a very young age to cook tasty vegetables and bread.

My grandfather fixed my monthly allowance at fifty rupees (approximately $1 Canadian in today's value.) If I spent more than that, then it was my tough luck! He would not give me any more money. In some situations, I had to borrow money from my friends. Some days I used to cry while walking with my canister on my head to my boarding house. I used to feel that I was short-changed every month. I had to buy fresh milk, fruits, and other supplies for the month, and fifty rupees was just not enough to meet my needs. This is the same situation that millions of people still face today.

A few months later, I got a break when the headmaster's wife started feeding me at least three times a week. I was doing chores for her, and she started treating me like her own family member, as she did not have any children of her own at that time. I was a favorite boy of the headmaster's family, and I spent two very good years with them. The headmaster's wife liked me very much, and I, in turn, lived without any financial problems. My headmaster was a volleyball champion, and he got me interested in playing volleyball with him on the team. I still like this game and play whenever I get a chance. I was definitely spending more than my allowance. I know my grandfather wanted to teach me to live within my means, but my allowance just never worked in the long run.

I spent two years in the boarding house, and I finished my grade 8 schooling. I also became used to residing alone and away from my family. The weekly visit was done by either walking or riding my bicycle. Since there were no paved roads on this route, I sometimes had to walk in the dark evenings. The pathway wound through dense hedges across a seasonal river.

One evening, I had to cross the river when it was at its full crest due to heavy rain. The water was up to my waist, and the river currents were quite powerful. I had my bag full of books and homework. I found it quite difficult to maintain my balance. Walking became difficult. The currents were swift, and I was moving away from the path. I decided to walk slowly, but it soon became apparent that this was not the right decision.

The desert riverbed had quicksand, and if you slowed down or tried to stop, even for a few seconds, you would sink. Suddenly a big log hit my body very hard. The flow of water was swift enough that it could have toppled me upside down, yet I didn't fall and managed to keep on walking. It was a good thing that I did not fall, or I would have been swept away. I was told later that a piece of log is good to hold on to but only in still not swiftly running water.

The river was about half a kilometers wide, and it took me more than twenty-five minutes to come to the shore on the other side. I had to take a diversion to join the main path due to soil erosion. The river made deep banks all over the sides of the area. It was famous for soil erosion during the rainy season. I continued my journey on to my village.

The moon was shining by now. It was very bright. The tall hedges along the path were creating creature-like shadows as I walked along. The evening temperature was getting cooler due to the rain, and there was a cool wind that was causing the leaves to flutter. I kept on walking briskly.

The hedges were creating an atmosphere as though someone was walking alongside me. Sometimes the moonlight would show a cluster of moving hedges that looked like many creatures walking alongside me. At one point I had to stop to look around just to make sure I was actually walking alone.

I picked up a stick as I could hear the hissing of a slithering cobra. There were plenty of cobras in and around the fields where this beaten path was formed. You need to keep walking to avoid a snake encounter. The cobra is a very good snake, if you do not cross its path. If it hears your footsteps, it will slither away from you with great speed. If the cobra is ahead of you, it will simply raise its hood, which causes a hissing sound to warn you to stay away from its path. I simply walked away from it.

The cobra will only strike when you confront it. If you happen to be in a confrontational situation, then you don't have a choice but to kill it with a blunt stick or other weapon. Failing that, the cobra will most likely kill you with a single bite to any part of your body. I knew how to avoid a cobra snake.

You can easily detect a snake inside of the hedges, as it keeps slithering and leaving its tracks in the sand. I used to see many on our farmland. Snakes are not seen as much these days due to paved roads and the noise of motor vehicles. However, I was constantly reminded to wear leather boots when making a trip to the farmland, and I always heeded this advice.

Sudden Illness

The schools were closed for two summer months – May and June – in the State of Rajasthan, where I was.

These two months bring extreme hot temperatures, sand storms, and blowing hot sand. Some days are so hot that you can loose your slippers on the road, as the black tar starts melting, and the road gets sticky.

First of all I picked up fever, which eventually turned into typhoid. A few days later, I picked up colitis and dysentery, which caused intestinal havoc.

My grandfather was very particular in seeing that I got cured quickly and that my ailment would not be prolonged. However, I was not so lucky at that time. The medicine was not working on me. He decided to switch my allopathic medicine to homeopathic pills with some restrictions on my diet. The homeopathic medicine was also taking too long to bring my fever down. I was loosing weight and getting weaker by the day. So he switched my homeopathic treatment to an Ayurvedic treatment, which is India's ancient herbal medicine system. I was getting herbal pills with restricted dietary meals. The fever continued. My eyes were getting weaker, and my pupils started dilating. My whole body started quivering with shivers.

My grandfather panicked, and he decided to call two medicine men also, and they tried to treat my fever with song and dance. These men had peacock feathers, which they waved over my body while singing songs loudly. One man was dancing while singing with another. Family members were all around me watching this treatment.

The song and dance treatment continued for three days. I was becoming unconscious during the treatment. My grandfather also hired two priests to sit in a corner and recite Mantras from Hindu scriptures for gaining health. He did not discontinue my medicines that I was given in the beginning.

This trial of treatments lasted a whole month. I was not sure which medicine worked on me, but I started feeling better after a month. My fever was gone, and somehow I was free from typhoid. But my troubles were not yet over. My colitis was acting up fiercely, and my stomach was hurting due to intestinal pain.

A new treatment started. This time, a doctor, who was quite experienced in ancient Indian Ayurvedic treatments, recommended that I be taken off all medications. He suggested that I go on a plain yogurt diet for three months. My grandfather knew the doctor well, so he concurred with the treatment. I was taken off all medications and all types of solid food, including grains, vegetables, and fruits.

Basically it was my body's internal cleansing process that was recommended for me. I was placed on this diet religiously, and for three months, I ate nothing but the plain yogurt three times a day. This was working under the doctor's supervision. My body started showing signs of recovery. The colitis started to vanish. I was completely free from colitis after three months. For the first week after the three-month period, I was kept on vegetable soups and then slowly introduced to grains. This brought me back to normal eating on a daily basis. I thought it was a miracle diet for me. Since then, I have never had a colitis attack. I would touch wood for that as the saying goes. However, I would not recommend this kind of treatment without a doctor's prescription.

My Maternal Uncle's Place

Although I missed two months of school, I finished junior high school and moved into my maternal uncle's (*mama ji* in Hindi) house. My uncle insisted that I complete my grade ten from the school in his town. Here I immensely enjoyed my two years of studies. I had no worries about cooking meals or maintaining my own household. I was often told that I was a dear addition to the family. My *naani* (maternal grandmother) and my *nana* (maternal grandfather) looked after me very dearly. My uncle treated me like his own son.

I used to walk to school, which was only about two kilometers away. The distance was shorter than the previous school, and there was a straight path. I never needed to come home late in the evening. At home, I had to thump over my nana's body for an hour every morning before going to school and every evening after coming back from school. He was suffering from arthritis and my mama ji prescribed this physiotherapy for him. My uncle was a doctor, who thought this would relax his muscles. I used to enjoy jumping on my nana's back, legs, arms, and shoulders everyday.

My nana found this therapy very soothing and helpful in relieving his arthritic pain. I also enjoyed walking along the edge of the roof of his second story house. The roof edge had no railings, and a free fall from the second story could have been fatal. But at my age, I was not really concerned about that. There was a big open window in the room, which had no screen or railing on the second story. This window used to be my favorite place to sit and to look down from a height of 25 feet.

I enjoyed my two years at my naani's place. The school only went up to grade 10, so I moved to a bigger city where I could carry on with my higher education. Once again, I would have to live on my own.

CHAPTER THREE
At a Young Age and My University Education

I moved to the big city of Jaipur, to complete grade 11 and then move on to my university education. I found a very loving family who rented one of their rooms to me. Although I arranged my own cooking, the lady of the house would often invite me to eat with the family. As the time went by, I was living there like a paying guest.

They had two children, a boy and a girl of my age. We were together most of the time. We attended the same school, and we used to play together and eat together. We practically lived in the same room. The parents were pleased with the arrangement. But as time passed on, one of the neighbors did not like me staying with the family. I'm not really sure why, but I was told that the girl and I might develop a relationship, which would have caused a big problem as we came from two different castes. The caste system does pose a big problem in society when it comes to marriages. It caused the parents' uneasiness, and I decided to relocate to another residence. I had completed grade 11 and was ready to begin my university education.

I encountered some financial problems due to my relocation and the high cost of a university education. Early on in my studies, two of my professors formed a very good opinion about my capabilities and good standing in their class. They had co-authored a book, and they asked me to market their book to all the colleges and universities in the state. With this assignment I found the opportunity for extensive travel and to meet academics and library personnel. Both professors paid me well, and I was able to complete my Masters in Economics and Public Administration.

Growing up images

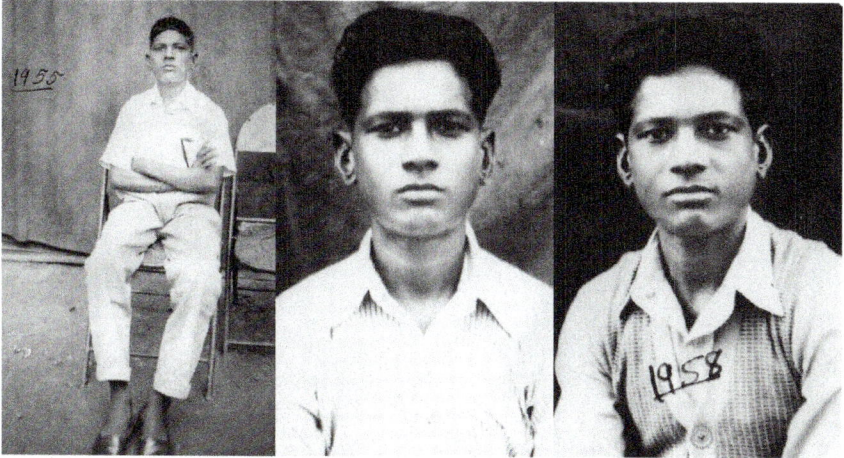

| My first photo at the age of 15, in 1955. | In 1957 | In 1958 |

| In 1959 | In 1960 | In 1961 |

1963. I am holding my Degree in Masters of Economics
and Public Administration from the University of Rajasthan, Jaipur, India.

During my time at the University of Rajasthan, I met a visiting professor, who inspired me to read about North America and especially about Canada to see if I would be interested in immigrating. I spent several hours every day at the university library, where I started reading extensively about Canada, European countries, and the United States of America. I was fascinated with the history of Canada, and at that time, I decided that I should go to Canada rather than to the United States. I found Canada more appealing. As I was about to plan my move to Canada, I decided to join in to the group pictures of our department so that it could stay in my albums when I moved after my graduation.

A group picture of our Public Administration class before graduation.

The class of students for Masters of Economics and
Public Administration at the University of Rajasthan.

In 1960, I joined a travel agency to make extra money. I enjoyed
working as an accounts officer, but I was also assigned travel duties to
look at the accounting systems in other travel agencies. I used to fly to
New Delhi quite often. The travel organizers at the agency were quite
friendly, and they used to provide me with descriptions of various cities
in North America. I also started researching details about Canada.

CHAPTER FOUR
Marriage and Starting Family Life

In 1961, my grandfather approached me to say it was now time for me to get married. He had already started contacting families in nearby towns to look for a girl so that he could arrange my marriage. I was only 21, but I was prepared to look at the girl my grandfather was selecting for me. He found a girl from our caste in a nearby town. He told me that this girl was the right match for me. I did not need to look elsewhere. She only had a high school education, but spoke well. She had a fair complexion and dressed well. She seems aggressive in her nature. Her father told me that she would fit in any and every situation with me. She would be a good companion and wife for me. Her name was Kamla. I did not want to question my grandfather. I thought that he was looking after my welfare and would not hook me up with the wrong girl. So I approved his selection. Later on, I told my friends that a girl had been chosen for me and very soon I would be betrothed.

My friends had no problem with the arrangement made by my grandfather, since they all had been married a year earlier, and their marriages had also been arranged by their parents. So I got married soon after it had been decided. On May 29th, 1962, I had a wedding party of approximately three hundred people. Kamla's father made arrangements to host the party in his town by providing every guest room and board for the three days of wedding celebrations.

The welcoming party of the bride's household received the guests with great pomp and show. A music band played songs, and people danced in the evenings. The feasts were elaborate with a number of special dishes for the guests. The priest performed a wedding ceremony that lasted all night. By the time the ceremony was over, both the bride and I had fallen asleep on the altar. The people woke us up at six o'clock in the morning. The last part of the ceremony was to take our vows. But as we had both been dozing, we simply reiterated sleepily what the priest was reciting. We did not have a clue about what was being said. After the wedding ceremony was over and I had returned home with Kamla, I noticed that her father had given me a gold chain, a gold ring, and a bicycle in the dowry. I did not care for that at the time. My friends, however, asked me later about the things I received. The bicycle came in handy for my commute downtown and to the railway station, where I used to go with my friends for coffee and snacks at two o'clock in the morning three times a week. The railway station was the only place where we could get good coffee at that time. On May 29th, 2012, Kamla and I celebrated 50 years together with our Golden Wedding Anniversary.

Kamla and I as a couple, long after our marriage.

After the marriage, I attended my convocation to receive my Masters of Economics and Public Administration in 1963 from the University of Rajasthan in Jaipur. My life took a turn from there onwards. Kamla and I rented a room in a family's home. The landlady was very friendly and protective of us as a young couple. Her husband was a lawyer. The travel agency where I was working also provided a scooter for my conveyance to and from my house. Kamla was in the landlady's care in my absence if anything was needed in an emergency. We both were enjoying married life. Kamla would ride the back seat of my scooter, and we scooted around the city in the evening, even in the rain and in storms, almost everyday.

In 1964, Kamla had a miscarriage, but with our landlady's help and support, any shock or grief was quickly forgotten at our age. On January 7, 1967, our first child was born in the hospital. We named our daughter Pinky. We chose this name since our city, Jaipur, was known as "the pink city". Being a young couple, that was the only name we could think of at the time. Kamla engaged herself with looking after her baby girl and her needs while nursing her. I was quite busy in my work and travel duties. Both Kamla and I shared our work to look after our little household.

CHAPTER FIVE
Journey to Canada

Back at the travel agency, in May of 1968, I came across a particular scholarship program at Brandon University in the province of Manitoba, Canada. That got me very interested in Canada. I applied for it, and I was successful in getting it. I had to wind up all my operations in Jaipur and prepare for a long journey to Canada.

My plan took a few months to organize. By this time, Kamla and I had been married for six years, and we had our second child on September 5, 1968. We named our second daughter Minky because it rhymed with Pinky. We could not think of another name because I was busy packing and organizing my travel to come to Canada. Kamla agreed with my move. She thought that my move to Canada would be a great step towards us settling in North America. I kept her informed on what I was reading about Canada. Both of us were in agreement to make such a move. I was to leave for Canada on September 7, 1968. Our daughter Minky was only two days old when I had to leave the country to come to Canada, as I was given very short notice to join Brandon University in Manitoba.

My travel manager was very happy that I was going abroad through a scholarship program. He decided to make my travel arrangements himself. In 1968, flight connections were not that frequent. The travel plan he came up with included transit stops in three countries with hotel and meals all included. These days it is difficult to find a travel plan like this. I took full advantage of my plan and visited three countries en route to Canada. I visited the city of London in England, Cairo in Egypt, and Rome in Italy.

I got busy packing my suitcase with the basic necessities that I needed for travel. I did not purchase too many things for the journey.

There were five more students already living in Brandon, as they had come a year ahead of me. Two of them were from Jaipur. I got a visit from the parents of one of the students, and they asked me if I could take a parcel for their daughter, who was studying in the same university. That way I would have someone to talk with as soon as I arrived in my new city in another part of the world. I thought it was a good idea to know someone from the same city who was already at the university I would be attending. Therefore, I agreed to carry a parcel for their daughter. A day later, I found out that the parents of this girl had left a full suitcase for me to take to her. I was not at home, and my wife started wondering if I would be comfortable carrying another piece of baggage with me. I was allowed to carry two pieces of checked baggage, so I agreed to take her suitcase. I am sure the parents, as well as their daughter, must have felt very happy to know that I was doing this favour for them.

A day later, I got another visit from a different family, and the father asked if I would give him 125 Indian rupees for $25 Canadian (the exchange rate was 5 rupees to a dollar at that time) from his son, who was also studying at Brandon University. This was a welcome visit for me, as I would receive Canadian dollars as soon as I arrived in Brandon, so I complied with his request.

Although I had graduated with my Masters in Economics and Public Administration with a specialization in International Banking, the scholarship I applied for and accepted was in Education. Manitoba needed teachers in the 1960s and had a new immigration policy that opened the doors for immigrants to come to Canada. This was a perfect opportunity for me to be in Canada.

I had to leave my wife and my two daughters behind in India to achieve this transition. It took two years for my wife and daughters to join me in Canada.

A requirement of the scholarship application form was to provide an essay on why I wanted to enter the field of Education. I used my experience from when I was in primary school to write this essay. I honestly wrote that when I was in primary school, one of my teachers was very strict and rude towards his students. He never spared a student who failed to complete his homework. He used to hit us with a rod or a broomstick if a mistake was made.

Unlike other teachers, he was a very popular teacher in the school. The reason for his popularity was that due to the fear he inspired, every student turned out to be intelligent and diligent later in life. He practiced corporal punishment like many other teachers. Though corporal punishment is against the law, it was practiced in schools. The teachers in rural schools still get away with it.

I knew that this method was wrong and that this was not the type of teacher I wanted to be. The qualities a teacher should demonstrate to his or her students should bring a positive impact on young minds. I wanted to find out myself by becoming a teacher. I wanted to search for a method of teaching, other than the one practiced in my country, to make every student intelligent and diligent without being in fear of punishment and while enjoying learning.

Going to another country to work was a priority and a personal goal for me. My teacher once told me that traveling abroad is a complete book, and that the one who has not travelled has only read one page of it.

During my travel from Jaipur to Manitoba, I had a very exciting journey. My travel itinerary was such that I got to enjoy five-star hotels and visit metropolitan cities in three different countries. I flew from the city of Jaipur to New Delhi on a local flight. This was the only flight I could bring my mother, maternal aunt, and my uncle with me to give them the experience of flying. I was very happy that they accompanied me on that flight. They probably would not get another chance to travel in a plane in those days.

After seeing me off at the New Delhi International Airport, they all travelled back to Jaipur by bus. When I was boarding my flight, all my family members bid me farewell. My grandfather was standing alone, sadly watching me leave the country. He had high hopes that after my university studies I would work in a high position and make a big name for my family. He did not want to see me go away like this. He would not even contribute towards paying for my travel.

On the other hand, he was happy that I was going abroad, as in those days very few people went abroad to live. He considered me one of the fortunate few people. I boarded my flight and looked through the window. I suddenly remembered that before boarding the plane I had forgotten to touch his feet, as touching the feet of our elders before leaving the family was compulsory in our tradition. I came running out of the plane and ran down the ladder. The air hostess was wondering what had happened after boarding the flight. She ran after me questioning why I was running from the plane, but stopped when she saw me touching my grandfather's feet. Everybody was standing by the plane. It was not like today when we go through a ramp and may not backtrack without a special security check. My family members took a special notice of my action and appreciated it very much.

My wife was still in the hospital on the day I was leaving Jaipur as our second daughter had been born two days earlier. However, Kamla took leave for a few hours from the hospital without consulting her doctor. This was a daring act on her part, but she was known for taking risks of any kind. I was surprised to see her at the airport just like everyone else who had come to see me off. Kamla had Minky all bundled up in one arm and Pinky by her side. It was very nice to see them before I left. Other family members were so happy to see them too. The plane started to roll on the runway while I kept on looking at them until we took off and left Jaipur airport.

I stayed in a five-star hotel in New Delhi, as there were no connecting flights until the next morning. I flew into London, England by Air India. Air India gave me a briefcase as a carry-on gift, which I still have today. It was a most comfortable flight up to London. The flight crew in the plane were very hospitable and they provided drinks, snacks, and meals, including authentic Indian food. It was a long flight, and I was feeling extremely anxious about the trip. After a nine-hour flight, we landed at Heathrow Airport. The agent arranged my ground transportation to a five-star hotel near post office tower, including all meals and gratuities. The travel arrangements had to be made this way because I could only receive US$8 from the Reserve Bank of India in those days. The university would provide room, tuition, and board for me once I arrived in Brandon.

I had all day and all night to look around London. Wherever I could sightsee for free was most appealing. The hotel room I stayed in was a gorgeous luxury room, and there was a buffet dinner in an elegant dining hall with a dress code, of course. This was a new experience for me, and I wished I had my family with me to enjoy as well

I left for Rome on a BOAC flight from London. I stayed in a hotel right in the downtown area. I had only an afternoon to spare in Rome. However, I was able to see quite a number of sights, including the famous Coliseum. In the evening, I went to a few bars and restaurants, as I was given free vouchers for meals and drinks. I boarded the plane the next morning for Cairo, Egypt. I got the perfect opportunity to tour the great pyramids of Egypt with a guided tour that started from my hotel.

It was a great experience staying in these cities, particularly since this was my first time out of India. I remember I was asked to purchase two bottles of liquor at the Rome and Cairo airports by airline hostesses traveling with me on the flights. I was not buying anything for myself. I was using my allowance after buying drinks for sightseeing. There was no question asked at the customs at any of these airports. I received $10 as a courtesy from each flight attendant for doing this favor for them. This action of mine earned me some extra money, which I desperately needed until I reached my destination.

CHAPTER SIX
Arrival in Canada

My flight safely touched Canadian soil at Montreal airport. I received my customs clearance at the entrance. The customs officer asked me similar questions to what I had been asked at the Canadian High Commissioner's office in New Delhi. The officer checked my documents carefully and put a stamp on my passport, approving my entry in to Canada. This was the happiest moment of my life. It was a new beginning of a new life.

I must say the reason I wanted to come to Canada, and leave my beautiful country of India behind, was what I had read about Canada when I was in grade eleven. My geography course in intermediate college had a section on North America. I was more attracted to Canada than the United States. Both countries were considered lands of milk and honey, but life in Canada seemed more peaceful. Canada also had free medical care, which was very appealing to me. The medical system in the United States was similar to that of India, where you would have to pay for treatment before even seeing a doctor.

The United States of America had over two hundred years of independence, while Canada was not even one hundred years old. The settlers and immigrants were still shaping the country's economic, social, and educational systems. I was fortunate that after my educational training was completed, I could immediately begin working as a teacher.

I was only 28 years old when I left India. India got her independence on August 15, 1947. She was only 21, when I left her in September

1968. I found that the job market was not very attractive for me even after I had completed my university education. I found that poverty was quite rampant in the cities as well as in the villages. Kamla was in full agreement that I should explore new frontiers for better fortunes.

My parents were living under the financial umbrella of my grandfather in a joint family system. My grandfather, even more than my parents, had very high hopes from me because I was the only one in nearby villages and towns who had earned a Masters degree from university. My younger siblings were still going to school, and I, being the eldest, was expected to take care of the family just like my grandfather did.

My level of education gave an added advantage to our family and was something to be proud of. My grandfather financed my education up to a certain extent, but my family wanted me to have a secure future. I was not born an entrepreneur, and I was not interested in engaging in our family business. I thought it would be better to try my luck outside of India, so I could provide a better life for my family and assist my parents back in India. Coming to Canada was the best opportunity to realize my hope for a better future.

As soon as I arrived, I was placed in the student residence of the university. The most important facility of the residence that I enjoyed was the shower in the bathroom. I found the residence a very attractive high-rise building. My room was in an annex. The rooms were clean and other amenities were easily available. Having a shower in the morning and evening every day was immensely enjoyable. The meals were served three times a day in the residence's dining hall. Life in the university was quite busy, as well as interesting, for the students, new and old.

CHAPTER SEVEN
Getting to Know the People

A day after I arrived, I was visited first by the girl who was expecting her baggage that I had brought all the way from India without any cost to her. She picked up her baggage and without any conversation left the residence. This looked like when you pick up your baggage from the carousal at the airport and leave. I found this very strange, since I was expecting her to converse and give me some information about the university and surroundings. I soon got busy in making my own arrangements for attending classes the next day, as well as organizing other activities for future sessions.

A few hours later on the same day, the gentleman walked in to meet and give me money. He sat down and got acquainted with me. He gave me a good description of the university and the city of Brandon and informed me that he would be teaching after graduation. He had a job lined up in a nearby town. After an hour, he gave me $25 Canadian in cash and left, promising to meet again. We kept meeting from time to time. He left the city after a year for further advancement and got married.

I never saw the lady who picked up her baggage again. My wife informed me that her parents also never went to visit her again, after I had left India and brought her baggage to her. About fifteen years later, I got a call from this lady, when she was looking for a job in the East after getting her PhD and I was working as school superintendent. I could provide her a number of options where she could establish herself. I lost touch after that. The gentleman I received Canadian money from got married in Toronto and moved back to India.

This is my first winter and first exposure to snow in 1968. I was very excited to see and feel snow for the first time.

Before I had arrived in Canada, the university sent me a very attractive brochure outlining the university's programs and with pictures of the buildings. The Education Department also informed me that there was a buddy system for new students. I was to be received by a fellow buddy selected by the university. My buddy received me as soon I arrived and greeted me at the university grounds. He showed me the university grounds and gave me an orientation of the residence where I was to stay, as well as the surroundings of the university within the city of Brandon. He took me to his home and introduced me to his parents and family members. He showed me around and made me feel at home in a new place.

As the town's people came to know that I was a new student from India, they started to invite me to their gatherings. My first visit was to a Rotary Club gathering. After an introduction session, I found myself on a question and answer panel. The people attending had a whole slew of questions about India. I was also able to satisfy their curiosity about the "Holy Cow". A few people asked me why the cow is sacred in India and known as a holy cow. I found this question amusing and easy to answer.

I quickly remembered what my grandfather used to tell me about cows. We used to have a lot of cows on our farm. One of my duties was to help see the cows to the field once every second day to ensure they were properly grazing and drinking water regularly around the pond. Two or three times during the year, our whole family used to put color on them to decorate them. We used to put a bell around the neck of the cows and tie saffron scarves on their horns.

I told the audience that there are two significant festivals in Hinduism. The first is *Krishna Janmasthmi* (the birthday of Divine Krishna), and the second is *Deepavali* (a festival of lights for the homecoming of Divine Rama after fourteen years in exile). My grandfather used to tell me a number of interesting facts about the cow's importance and about how to worship and celebrate these festivals. He also explained why the cow is considered a sacred animal among Hindus.

The Hindus' veneration for the cow dates back several thousands of years. The Hindu god Krishna was very fond of cow's milk and its butter. And the cow was his dearest animal friend. He would gladly spend all of his time with the cows in the grazing field. Krishna in his childhood would go and steal butter from nearby homes .The village girls known as *Gopies* (cowgirls in the town of Gokul, where Krishna was raised) would feed him butter out of their house in order to listen to him play his flute, as he was the lord of the flute and its divine music.

One of the tenets of the Hindu philosophy is non-violence, and the practice to protect and revere cows takes the form of an absolute prohibition against killing a cow. From the religious point of view, the bull is the sacred ride of Lord Shiva, who is the third member of the triumvirate (the lord of destruction and re-creation). The first is Vishnu, the lord of preservation, and the second is Brahma, the creator of this universe.

We may not think of a bull without the existence of a cow. The farmers use oxen to plough and bullock carts to transport the crops. Cow dung is still used as an organic fertilizer in the fields and cooking fuel in village homes.

Cow's milk is also healthy and light. When a cow dies, its hide has many uses in the economy. Cows are given special respect in Hindu families. Cow products are often used in Hindu religious celebrations and rites. For instance, a particle of cow dung and a drop of cow's urine, mixed with sweets, honey, and curd, is put on the tongue of a bride and groom during the wedding ceremony. The saints and priests living in solitude keep cow shelters to protect them from slaughter-houses. Cows are still offered as a dowry in the villages. When a person dies, a cow is donated so that the person will easily cross the river of mud, insects, reptiles, and blood in hell by holding onto the cow's tail as the cow can swim through any hurdles.

A cow has so many uses that Mahatma Gandhi used to call it a poem of pity.

The gentle nature of a cow is often attributed to a woman, who has a tremendous amount of tolerance. The cows may wander or park on busy sidewalks or streets in the downtown of any city in India. You may even see one or two cows sitting around with an audience listening to a Hindu preacher.

Lord Krishna descends on the face of this earth as the incarnation of God to protect the cows as soon as he sees that their elimination is imminent or that too much cruelty is laid upon them. My grandfather told me that if you rub the skin of a cow seven times regularly for forty days, you may acquire a pair of divine eyes to behold Krishna, and if you put your head on the back of a cow, your headache will disappear. If an expectant mother drinks cow's milk for twelve days or more, she may give birth to a child with divine qualities.

It is said that worshiping a cow means worshiping the God himself. If one does not worship cows, then it means that God is not worshipped or the worship is incomplete. It is said that when a cow is buried in a field, you don't need manure within two acres of the skeleton. Therefore, a cow is very useful even after it dies. The cow's urine has potent medicinal value and is used in Ayurvedic (ancient Indian herbal) medicine. It has antiseptic qualities.

The audience was quite fascinated to hear this long answer filled with details about the Hindu religion and the importance of cows for Hindu families. I was treated like a celebrity that evening.

I was invited to another meeting with a lot of students, teachers, and parents, where they asked a number of questions about India and Indian society. The questions were quite interesting, but what Indian people would consider private. However, I quickly learned that people in the West are much more open. I've listed the questions below, but not my responses.

Do you like kissing your wife? How long have you been married? Would you want to date me? Why did you name your children Pinky and Minky? What is a punchline? What kind of music do you like – rock and roll, classical, jazz, or what? Where do you come from originally? What do you think of sex? Does your wife speak English? Do you have a nickname? Why do you have a funny accent? What kind of clothes do the people wear in India? Do you like NHL hockey? Could you tell us about life in your homeland? Do you like Canada?

I was a bit nervous in the beginning, as I did not have the answers to some questions – specifically related to Canadian hockey, my nickname, and my accent. Some questions I had hard time to answer because of my cultural shyness, such as those related to sex. However, I was able to deal with the questions as best as I could. I began by saying that people in the West find our system of education vastly different as the children in India were not allowed to express themselves in the classroom or outside as much as here in the West.

People also had limited knowledge about Indian customs. For example, the Indian custom of sharing one's food was a new experience carried out by the daily lunch pools by me with other Indian friends. When I became a teacher, a young child in grade one asked me an amusing question: Do students in Indian schools have pencils to write with?

I also gave them some insight about the role of women in India. Women play an important role in keeping the family together and keeping customs and culture maintained in society. I spoke about the advantages and disadvantages of the joint family system where three generations live under one roof.

The Hindu arranged marriage system is another custom I explained. The parents and their friends go together to find families who have boys and girls of marriage age and who are of the same caste and background. Both parents call a Hindu priest in their homes to match the horoscopes of the boy and girl for the purpose of lifelong suitability. The bridegroom sees his bride for the first time in the mirror during the marriage ceremony, unless his close friends can arrange a meeting before the wedding. Child marriages that were once acceptable have been abolished, and now the minimum age for girls is 18 years and for boys it is 21 years. The husband is treated like a god by Indian women.

Seventy-five per cent of India's population lives in small villages where the veil system is prevalent. It is a fearful system from ancient times.

Superstition plays a major role in daily life of families in Indian society. People of every caste worship their own god. Society does not give much significance to divorce between a husband and wife. The education system needs to bring changes in society.

The people present at this meeting enjoyed the information, and we shared a lot about each other's customs and traditions. I also learned a lot about Canada, and some things I learned the hard way.

My new friends gradually arranged a number of meetings, which I attended in various church groups and enjoyed a lot. I found the people very friendly and socially interesting. My friends made me feel at home, wherever we went together. I was also learning the customs of Western society. I made good friends with a number of young people, male and female alike, so that I could easily move around the student community and the community at large. I enjoyed the campus life to the fullest like any other young student at the university and in the city.

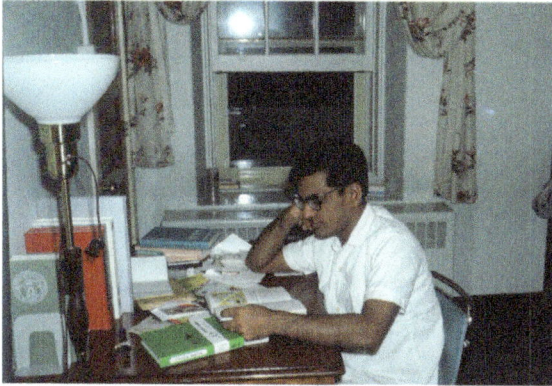

I got busy in my studies as soon as
I enrolled at the University in Brandon.

I am visiting a family.

I am reciting a poem.

I am playing a game of shuffleboard.

I am participating in a play.

I have seen snow for the first time.

I decided to sink in it for fun.

I enjoyed the background of snow-covered
trees and snow everywhere.

One day I went to a restaurant with my friends, along with couple of invited female friends. We had a delicious meal in a fancy restaurant. When the time came to pay the bill, I felt little uneasy, as I only had enough money to pay for my own meal. I had the impression that people in the West normally paid for their own meal.

I soon came to know that if you invite any female friend to dine with you, then you have to pay, as this is then considered a date. I was married and did not consider this a date. I was told if you don't have money to pay the bill, you could be asked to wash dishes until you make enough money to pay the bill. In order to get out of this embarrassment, I had to phone my friend at the residence to come to the restaurant and bring some money to pay our bill. My friend came and helped me pay the bill. We took care of the situation and promised never to make a mistake like that again.

I composed a poem for each of my friends to mark the occasion and to remember the situation. I composed the poems very quickly in the restaurant to please the guests. I had a real knack for composing poetry from back home in those days.

Poem 1

Very first glance at black eyes of a white senorita,

So bright inside as black clouds have thunder light,

Unstable between sharp brows that billowing pearl,

Like wondering dove leaping unsatisfied.

Effected me to pause, to think, to be cool, and not,

To release arrow, let dove go in her own style.

With fine foot, pride, scarlet lips, high head,

Quivering limbs full of life and smile.

Look friends! Those, dagger-like eyes as spy,

Turned, sparkled, and stabbed right in heart.

Search and see the spot, five senses in slots,

Murmuring day and night of this bloodshed.

My efforts to console entirely failed and,

In-spite of utmost cry and severe pain,

That obstinate heart wants damages full,

Nothing! but, in terms of a dagger, the same.

All, fellow beings! Find, the master of heaven or hell,

God or man, I don't care, make a point well.

I want a judgment for this assault,

Just listen! If any eye stabs you, it is none of your fault.

Poem 2

Campus, lounge, link, and hall,

Dining, walking, or playing ball,

I behold verily with my eyes,

An individual! Rich with smile.

Smile and smile at East,

And turns to assimilate with the West.

When wind breaths this flower of,

Hope – no melancholy even least.

Autumn, winter, rain, and spring,

Summer and fall like to swing.

One knows what all in weather,

Whether or not you believe,

Nature is summed-up when,

I see and talk to "Heather".

Poem 3

An individual not known,

To me and John, even now,

After seeing, meeting, talking,

Joking and so on,

No one has seen inside the dearest,

Solace to love and nearer,

Known or unknown,

I urge the creator to take away the instinct,

Meeting and departing, heartening stroke,

When Sue will be away like,

A dearest robin has flown.

Poem 4

To your surprise my friend!

There was a time, when

I was stopped to praise the reality

Like, I committed a crime.

In a home among family,

My senses were busy to find.

The reality and a marble statue,

Are, whether on the same line.

Real was high, charming, unspeakable,

But cruel, one has to define.

People snap the real and turn to statue,

What to realize is beyond my mind.

Home, parents, kids, and I,

A real individual among, but shy,

Frank but fail, unable to run,

Trying to talk with down lids on eye.

My visit, surprise you nor I

Free from the crime.

In your mini, I behold,

Verily, you were sublime.

My buddy was my guide to show me places and things and to make my life easier in a new city and new country. One day he took me to a local nightclub. I sat with a group of classmates and his friends close to the stage where strip dancers performed. The music was loud and patrons were busy drinking, talking, and laughing. There was a pillar in front of my chair where I was sitting.

When the dancer appeared on the stage, the pillar obstructed my view as other people were also moving their heads. Out of temptation, I got up and stood up on my chair to have a peek. In a flash, people started to look at me rather than the dancer. My buddy pulled me down to sit in my chair. He told me that no one does this, and the patrons and security might think I was trying to go on the stage to accompany the dancer. I still make it a topic of conversation and joke about it during parties.

I was offered a part-time job at the university library for extra pocket money. One day, I had to go for a haircut downtown. I was used to an old-style barber's shop back home. I entered into a salon. The front chamber was occupied with ladies in hair dryers and curlers going in plastic helmets all around. I waited a while, and the receptionist came from behind the partition. She asked if I needed any help. I realized quickly that this was not a place where a man could get a haircut. I simply used an excuse by saying I thought my wife came to this salon and left. I felt somehow I was just not at the right place!

I wrote a poem to remember this experience and decided to recite it at a friend's farewell party.

Poem 5: Funny Experience

From campus to strand, while walking, I told my friend,

Two months over, it's getting bad,

Look hair scolding my head.

Go ahead! Soon came his reply

A place to see, while roaming and try.

While entering saw reception,

On steps got some new conception.

I removed slams amber, oh my god! Sneaky chamber.

How dare to back and cry,

Started to count my stars in the sky.

Fragrance and perfume, heaven scent I presume.

Models were inside, full of style, curly ringlets, and smile.

Clean wall mirrors, shampoo, and cleaners;

Chain of chairs and slots, helmets of astronauts;

You know what I mean, of this holy place very clean,

Of chanting eye view, which I never knew;

Oh how nice to see you, a soft voice,

Not to rejoice, from curtain, churned my heart, throbbing,

Split apart, and I vomited, "Thank You."

Sorry I was sarcastic, to me but fantastic.

Unbelievable presence, embarrassing moments;

I jumped all the steps, Ladies and Gentlemen,

It was a beauty parlor – Amen.

It was the month of October, and you could feel the cold weather of the fall season. The trees had different colors with pretty leaves, which I really enjoyed seeing. At the end of the month, children were very excited to welcome the festive occasion of Halloween. I had never heard of this festive day, which falls on October 31 every year. Children are dressed-up in very special costumes to wake up the spirits and go door-to-door for candy, saying "Trick or Treat". They collect bags full of treats from house to house. They go home late in the night and count their candies with great pride. The little children go with their parent as escorts so that they do not miss the treats. I also joined other households to distribute candies to the little ghosts.

Poem 6

Among dead leaves tonight;

Witches, elves, and those spirits;

Ghoul, goblin, spooks, and gnomes;

Nitya, as host in between,

Has to dance at this Halloween.

I had two visiting professors from England come to teach a course in practical communication skills in the classroom. The professors assigned practical case studies as part of the course. I selected a case study where I would have to conduct interviews with a number of car dealers. I was to collect their responses and put them together to further analyze the communication pattern. I really enjoyed this case study.

Here's my narration of the case study.

I happened to go to a camping trailer lot. The campers in the lot were so neat and compact that I actually felt like buying one. As I made a move to have a closer look at the camper, a salesperson approached and asked me if there was anything he could help me with. I just felt like buying one but was not prepared to buy one. The salesman's sudden presence made me ask him if there was a smaller unit in the showroom I could look at?

My question was like an answer to his question. There was one unit standing in a corner. The salesman lifted this unit by himself and pulled it over by my side. The camper was very light, and he wanted to prove this by carrying it over. This was the smallest unit left to be sold, he said. I asked if it was complicated to put it up in a campground. The salesman said, "No, it is very simple to put up." He started to demonstrate further that first you unscrew the four legs and let them drop to touch the ground. "You have to ask someone else to hold the front end to bring all four legs to be the same length.

You have to screw the legs tight in place so that the camper stays in one place firmly. You need to open the latches from both sides; here is the crank, and you need to crank it up to lift the canopy up. This will prepare your roof. You need to unfold both sides of the camper, and two shafts will stick out. You pull the latch out, and here you will have two little steps in the centre open up for you to go in and out. Now go inside and see how spacious the camper is. The camper in the box looks small."

My next question was if the canvas of the camper was water repellent. He replied, "Oh yes, you better believe it. The camper also has three years warranty. The canvas is well treated. You will sleep like a baby inside, even if it's raining cats and dogs outside."

I was going to quit asking questions, but not abruptly. I asked another question about if it was safe to cook inside the camper. He said it is not advisable to cook in a camper of this material. I thought I better ask him about the cost of the unit before I kept on asking other questions.

When he quoted the cost price of the unit, I had no choice but to quit, and did not bother asking another question. I told him I needed more time to consider buying, and I would drop by again. The whole thing was a misunderstanding. If I had clarified my intentions in the beginning, then I would have actually interviewed him for my class rather than him thinking I was a customer. Unfortunately, I did not get the right type of information for my assignment and case study, but I did get a lot of information about campers.

When I came to Canada, my spoken English was not perfect. I had taken my graduate courses in English in India. However, my degrees were awarded in the Hindi language. My professors in India also spoke with an accent. I did not have many friends or classmates with which to practice my conversational English. But I did practice on my own through tutorials, and I managed to achieve near perfect mastery of the English language before arriving in Canada. In order to have a fluency in speaking English, I had to engage in conversational English within social groups and classes on the university campus. My Canadian friends quickly taught me a conversational and slang vocabulary to be used from time to time. I learnt slang and vocabulary along with figures of speech that I never had heard before.

Are you interested in joining our beard (show business)?

That big baboon (big man, strong) was fatigued.

The big brass (boss) fired us all for not completing our work.

The kids had free time that came out as birchen (good time).

She boasted (shoplifted) a pair of diamonds.

Dig those broads (girls).

Hey you, you got any booze (beer or liquor)?

Would you lend some bread (money)?

If the cops get you, you are busted (your reputation is ruined).

Save two bits (a quarter).

So that's your bag (thing).

The boys are cheesed off (angry).

She is the best chick (girl) in the school.

Isn't she a city slicker (person from a town or city)?

Cool it (keep calm or take it easy), lady.

I am cooped up (fed up) in this room.

The chicks were crabby (in a bad mood) after the game.

You must be cracked (stupid).

Lets take a crash (sleep).

My crash pad (place to sleep) has exotic colours all around it.

Boy, you can make a darn (shucks) mess.

Can you dig (understand) it?

It did not take very long for me to get into the mainstream with the professors, classmates, and social groups in the university, along with my friends, to start using common expressions, as well as academically driven conversation.

I was quite successful due to the fact that I started maintaining a logbook and notes on important topics of discussion among various groups during my study time. I was quite determined to succeed here. In fact, I started listing common expressions that I had not used and started practicing whenever I could. I am not sure where you can find the following expressions in one place, but I kept listing them as I came across them. For example: A storm of protest, a grain of salt, a grain of truth, a foggy idea, a wave of distrust, seeds of envy, a blushing bride, a sea of mud, a crying need, an aching void, a bouncing baby, bed of roses, a bird's eye view, all his geese are swans, a wild goose chase, a lame duck, a bird in the hand, round robin, showered with good wishes, a ripple of laughter, a sunny disposition, misty-eyed, clouded thoughts, town's mushroom growth, dead tired, death at every window.

A head of cabbage, to reach at the foot of the mountain, loosing our heads, the hands of the clock, the face of a cliff, the head of the state, the body of the letter, the mouth of the river, the eye of a needle, the foot of the class, a skeleton in the closet, a bone to pick, to make no bones about the matter, hand to mouth living, tongue in cheek, hand in glove, the cold shoulder.

We read to kill time, he flew upstairs, she brushed past me, the police combed the city, he ate his words and swallowed his pride, the rain drummed on the roof, he was greeted by thunderous applause, a car that eats up gas, to burn up the gap, pedestrians swarming across the intersection, a buttermilk sky, a fiery temper, he is always in hot water, a knot of people on the corner, the hood of a car, a good road bed, a bottleneck in the traffic, a traffic tie-up, to weave in and out of traffic, Richard the lion-hearted, he won by a landslide, her greeting was chilly, their laughter died at once, my heart sang, her gown trailed in the dust, a thought flashed through my mind, poverty has sharpened his wits.

I must master these French verbs, the waves slapped against the side of the boat, they treaded their way through the undergrowth, a veil of fog hung over the city, his buzz saw voice droned on, pale and thin, she was a ghost of her former self, death whispered in his ear, a smiling moon peeped out of the clouds, the guests sat down to a groaning table, summer lies smiling in the sun, we saw the frowning barrel of his gun, the pen is mightier than the sword, about a mile up the road was a camp of redcoats, the captain ordered all hands on deck, we were mad with joy, I have told you thousands of times not to interrupt me, they have tons of money, he missed him by a mile, she wept buckets with every disappointment.

I kept collecting and listing a number of words and phrases from various magazines as I came across them to keep my vocabulary strong in my daily life in Canada:

Putting old wine into new bottles, to hang a millstone by his neck, to hide your light under a bushel, to kill the fatted calf, set thine house in order, to heap coals of fire upon his head, cast thy bread upon the waters, seeing through a glass darkly, a house divided against itself, to grind the faces of the poor, unstable as water, thou shall not excel, the Lord is my rock and my fortress, our days on the earth are as a shadow, the words of his mouth were smoother than butter, but war was in his heart, we like sheep have gone astray, his enemies shall lick the dust, they that saw in tears shall reap in joy, he shall come down like rain upon mown grass, riches certainly make themselves wings, thou art weighed in the balance and found wanting, my days are swifter than the weaver's shuttle, man is born unto trouble as the sparks fly upward, as many as the sand which is by the sea, in the mouth of the foolish is a rod of pride, the way of the slothful man is as a hedge of thorns, but the way of the righteous is made plain.

I was getting fluent in the English language, especially in picking up local vocabulary and slang. One needs to understand slang in order to understand others' humor, and that's what I understood very quickly. I had no problem in English literature, whatsoever. I was very good in spelling in my early schooling in India.

I had a great time at the Faculty of Education at Brandon University. I completed the Secondary Education 1 Diploma, which qualified me to teach up to high-school courses in Manitoban schools.

I graduated in May 1969.

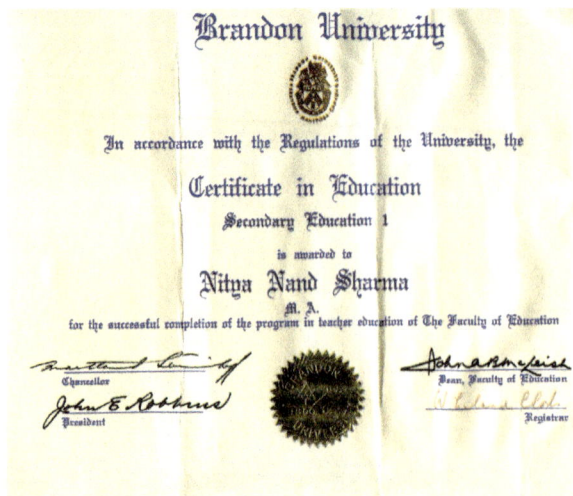

Here is my Certificate in Education-Secondary Education 1.

There was a recruitment season in April, and school superintendents from various school divisions were visiting universities and setting up recruiting fairs. The superintendent of education from the Department of Indian and Northern Affairs Canada (INAC) interviewed me during this recruitment drive and offered me a teaching position for one year in Cross Lake. I was totally excited to accept the assignment to teach in a Northern setting for the first time in my life. I thoroughly enjoyed my teaching assignment in Cross Lake.

I was one of four teachers living on the third floor of the school building in separate quarters, with a common kitchen. We jointly agreed that the two female teachers would cook the meals, and the two male teachers, including myself, would do the dishes and keep the kitchen clean before going to our quarters. We became good friends, besides being colleagues with this arrangement.

I became very interested in school activities. I volunteered to edit the school newsletters and copy them on an old Gestetner printer (a kind of copying machine), the only type available in the school; to send letters to the parents; to coordinate teacher-parent meetings; and to organize extra-curricular activities for the students of all grades. Both the principal and vice-principal of the school were quite pleased that I was demonstrating leadership skills in the school activities. I also published a booklet to commemorate Manitoba's centennial year, which was well received by all.

My teaching assignment in Cross Lake was suddenly interrupted after four months due to an unfortunate fire, which engulfed the entire high school building in a matter of hours. I was moved south with a different assignment. Since then, I have worked in other communities as a teacher and as a principal of a school. In later years, I worked as a guidance counsellor, assistant superintendent, education superintendent, and in various acting positions. My one-year term later changed in to a permanent position until I retired after 31 years with the department. My work life needs a new book, which I may write separately.

It was the month of November in 1968. I was going to witness the winter season in Canada. The most fascinating thing about this season for me was the snowfall. It would be the first time I would see snow. The snow falls after all the leaves fall from the trees. The leaves fall after they have changed into various colors during the autumn season. The winter and its snowfall lead to four other seasons. All four seasons of Canada provide very unique climatic conditions. I will mention this phenomenon as I go along. I was quite moved by the sight of a snowfall. I even wrote a few poems about this during the first year of my stay in Brandon.

Poem 7: Snow

Snow is a big cap over the land, and it's hard to pick it all by hand;

Snowball, we can throw, and have a fight; have fun, it's light.

When you touch it's cold, but easy to hold.

It covers power lines, but grapes will not grow in vines.

To me, snow is a white cloud, and people of it are very proud.

It falls on cars, homes, and on you, bringing flakes,

You can fill your jars, as it fills ponds, rivers, and lakes.

When I see snow all around, it looks like sugar on the ground.

I have to touch snow, because it gives a blow to laziness, and for those who are slow.

Snow looks like cream spilling out, and the kids like to play and shout.

Snow is very cold, for some it is old, for some it is new, the reason,

I never knew.

The hills wear a crown of snow, not looking low,

In the snow we can slide, one by one or side by side.

When snow falls on the ground, it is everywhere found.

We love throwing balls after it falls,

Everyone shouts snow, we like it falling slow.

Snow falls from the sky, and the birds fly sky high.

During my first year at university, I had saved enough pocket money to purchase a camera. I purchased a nice camera, which took slides as well as photo prints. A short time later, I also purchased one 8-mm silent movie camera along with a tape recorder to synchronize the sound and a projector to watch what I filmed. I took hundreds of photos as well as made some films. This was a new adventure for me. I started making good films with sound.

I also bought a car with an automatic transmission, although I learned how to drive a car on a manual shift tractor at my friend's farm near Brandon. This was my first car.

I was driving downtown one day at a pretty slow speed. There were two cars behind me. One of the cars wanted to pass me in a hurry, but the driver was unable to pass my car as there were cars approaching from the other side. The young driver somehow managed to squeeze through the traffic. As he came closer to my car, he opened the window and showed me a finger. I did not know at that time what he really meant by showing a finger. However, I thought he might be pointing something out to me. When I didn't make anything out of it, I simply cranked down my window and showed him two fingers. He just smiled and sped away. I kept thinking, "What if he showed me all five fingers?" I probably would have shown him my fist.

This incident reminded me of the classical story of the great poet Kalidasa of India. A king's daughter named Vidyotma, commonly known as Vidya (a very learned girl), would marry any suitor only if he defeated her in an epic based debate. If the suitor was defeated, he would be beheaded by the king's orders. A number of suitors were beheaded during the debate. It was actually getting out of hand, and a good number of intelligent and learned young boys were being beheaded simply because they were not beating her intelligence. Finally a group of pundits decided to fetch a foolish man to debate with her. Several king's guards went around looking for an idiot. In one place, they saw a young man who was sitting on a branch of a large tree and was sawing off the same branch he was sitting on. No one could be more foolish than this man, they thought.

When Vidya saw this man on the stage for the debate, she showed him one finger, meaning that there is only one God. But Kalidasa thought she wanted to poke his one eye. So he showed her his two fingers, meaning he would poke both of her eyes, if she dared. Vidya felt defeated knowing that God resides in every soul. Therefore, God and the soul are one.

In her sequence of questioning, she now showed him her five fingers, meaning the five elements (ether, water, fire, sky, and wind) that are essential for life. But Kalidasa thought she wanted to slap him.

So he showed her his fist, meaning he would punch her face if she slapped him. Vidya again felt defeated, knowing that life would not exist unless all five elements were joined together in one. So the king declared Kalidasa the winner and married Vidya to him. However, on the night of honeymoon, Kalidasa could not correctly pronounce the word "camel" in Sanskrit. Vidya realized that she had married a fool. She humiliated him and left him on his own.

But Kalidasa was in love and wanted Vidya badly. So he prayed and meditated upon Saraswati, the goddess of learning, who appeared in front of him to give him a boon. All Kalidasa asked was for Vidya to stay with him permanently as his wife. Goddess Saraswati granted him his wish.

Kalidas from here on studied intensely, and he became the master a epics. He wrote four literary epics that are now studied in higher learning in India. Kalidasa got his wish in its entirety, as Vidya came back to him as his wife.

I ended up telling my buddy that he never taught me about people showing the finger while driving. My buddy told me that sometimes you have to pick up things on your own as you experience other people's behavior. I learned quickly that the young fellow in the car was not showing me *a* finger, but actually giving me *the* finger for driving too slow.

I had already received my driver's license in the North. I had fun driving in Canada, as the roads were quite wide and there were divided highways. I even drove to Toronto and Niagara Falls in the summer of 1969 with a friend of mine. I made a good movie of this trip, which we still enjoy with the family.

One day in Brandon, I had to go do fieldwork from the students' residence, and I had to use my car for the day. I returned to the office the next day as an RCMP officer came knocking on the door asking for me. He showed me a car registration plate and asked if this was my car. My answer was affirmative. Then, he informed me that there was a green streak and a big scratch on the back side of another car that was parallel parked next to mine. He also said that the same green mark was found on my front steel bumper. The officer found that while pulling back, I had scratched the paint of the car parked on the left to mine. Therefore, he had to give me a ticket. I had no answer, as the paint matched on both cars. This was my first parking mistake. Manitoba did not have auto insurance through MPIC at that time. The officer, however, gave me only a warning ticket, and I expressed my gratitude to him for that. I do not want to repeat that again as long as I drive.

One day I was driving carefree from Dauphin to Brandon without looking at the speedometer. A police car was right behind me with its siren flashing, telling me to pull over. I stopped my car and asked if I had done anything wrong. The officer pointed out that I was driving 90 kilometers in an 80-kilometers zone. He also said that I had not been paying attention to the flashing siren and it took me too long to pull over. I apologized to the officer and made a plea that my speedometer perhaps was acting up. The officer looked at me and warned me that this time he would let me go, but I should pay attention on the highway to the speed limit. I thanked the officer and drove away. This was my first highway mistake, and it made me cautious to watch the speed limit whenever I drive. Although I kept driving carefully, I eventually got a speeding ticket on the same highway a month later. The police officer asked me a couple of questions, and one of them was if I liked Canada. I told him that I very much liked Canada, but I did not like the ticket he had just handed over to me. He smiled and left.

CHAPTER EIGHT
Sponsoring the Family

I could not wait to bring Kamla, Pinky, and Minky to Canada from India. I got my permanent residency after completing my one year of training to be a teacher and one year of teaching. I was now in a position to sponsor them to join me. I was feeling homesick after spending almost two years in Canada without seeing my family.

I decided to go back home to see the family, as well as to arrange their immigration to join me in Canada. It was the summer of 1970, when the World Trade Exhibition was taking place in Osaka, Japan. I decided to coordinate my travel itinerary to coincide with the visit via Osaka to India. I was able to stay in several cities on my way to India.

I took sightseeing tours and had a first-hand experience of seeing the Trade Exhibition in Osaka. I visited the cities of Vancouver, San Francisco, Honolulu, Wake Island, Tokyo, Osaka, Taipei, Hong Kong, Beirut, Paris, and London. I spent my time visiting the tourist attractions in these cities. Unfortunately, I lost my carry-on bag at the airport in Tokyo. I had a good collection of pictures and slides of Pearl Harbor in the city of Hawaii, Wake Island, Beirut, and Taipei in Taiwan. I had no other pictures of these places to show anyone, except a few that I saved in a separate bag. However, by the time I reached India, I had a good collection of souvenirs from various places.

As I landed at Jaipur airport, all my family members, parents, grandfather, relatives, and friends greeted me, as it was my first time coming home from abroad. Everyone was curious to see how I would look and act after a couple of years.

Kamla came to touch my feet. I had almost forgotten the Indian custom that a wife touches her husband's feet when you meet or depart. I bent to lift her and said, "Okay, okay that's fine," which became a laughing matter while I stayed in India. My two years of absence made her look different or maybe I looked at her differently. But it was a very sweet homecoming for me.

It was a very pleasant get together for everybody. Pinky was three, and Minky was two years old by now. I spent a good amount of time with my family in Jaipur and was able to facilitate the paperwork for Kamla and the girls' Canadian immigration visa. I had to leave after six weeks, as I had to come back to my job and send sponsorship papers for Kamla.

Kamla needed to come to Canada soon. She was going through tough times in the village. We had two girls, and my younger brother had a son at that time. The son of my brother was favored over our daughters, and the family members, as well as village ladies, were showing Kamla their indifference towards her. At one point, Minky fell from a one-story house and fractured her arm, but no one paid attention. Kamla was taking her to a bone specialist for a massage on a daily basis. She did it for almost six months, even when it was cold or raining. While she was gone, she left Pinky with a potter, who was our neighbor and a kind person.

Kamla's elder brother was also a very kind person, and he would pick up Kamla to take her to her parents' home whenever she wanted to live in peace and away from my village. Both Pinky, and Minky were in good hands with their mother. I was sending money for them through an agent in Toronto to make sure that they were not deprived of any necessities. Sometimes the agent would fly to Jaipur from New Delhi to deliver the money in person. This kept Kamla and the girls in comfort, as well as free from economic problems. In October 1970, Kamla received sponsorship and immigration papers for them to come to Canada.

Kamla

Kamla's sitting photo.

Kamla standing in the lawn.

Kamla, before departing India.

A farewell party of friends and relatives at the
Jaipur Airport before boarding the flight to come to Canada.

Pinky before coming to Canada.

Kamla left our family members behind. We would visit them from time to time as the situation permitted us over the years. We keep their pictures with us in Canada as a memory only.

Photo of my grandfather and grandmother.

Photo of Kamla's father.

Photo of Kamla's mother with children.

Photo of my father and mother.

Kamla Arrives in Canada with Pinky and Minky

Kamla and the girls finally did join me a year later as landed immigrants. They had an exciting trip to Canada. Kamla received intensive tips in India for traveling overseas and for living in North America, especially living permanently in Canada. One retired Canadian teacher in Jaipur provided Kamla with an elaborate orientation session before she left India. Kamla received a lot of information about Canadian society, food habits, shopping, culture, and people. Kamla told me that the Canadian lady even taught her how to set up a dining table, use cutlery, dance at a function, and move around in society in general. At one point, Kamla said the orientation was boring for her and she lost interest. She had high hopes that she would not abandon Indian ways of living while still assimilating with Canadian culture.

Kamla successfully and safely arrived at the international airport in Winnipeg in the middle of January 1971. I was there to receive them inside the terminal. I drove them from the airport. On my way to Portage La Prairie, the highway was very slippery. At one point, I suddenly applied the brakes, and my car slipped in such a way that it started spinning. The car made two turns on the highway, and the brake lights reflected like a police car was approaching me with its dome light on. It was 8pm and snowing. Kamla and the girls screamed on their first car ride in Manitoba. They were petrified and started asking if I actually knew how to drive in Canada. I had to explain to them that the icy roads make driving treacherous on the highways and sometimes braking makes the car spin. I made them feel comfortable after stopping the car on the side of the highway.

I had already told them that they would see plenty of snow and feel very cold during the three or four months of winter. Once we arrived at home, they started enjoying the snow.

Kamla arrives in Canada with our daughters,
Pinky and Minky, at our first house in the middle of January 1971.

I am sitting with Pinky and Minky after they arrived in Canada.

Kamla with Pinky and Minky, already playing in the snow,
that they saw for the first time.

In 1973, Kamla was pregnant again. She started having some problems during her pregnancy. I was teaching up north in an isolated

community, where there were no medical facilities. I had to bring her to the nearest town called Pine Falls to see the doctor for periodic medical check-ups. At one point, Kamla was losing a considerable amount of blood, and she had to receive blood transfusions during the pregnancy. At the seventh month, I had to bring Kamla to Portage La Prairie city, where she lived with a close friend till her delivery. The doctor told her that she had a rare blood type that is found only in Rhesus monkeys, which makes her bleed profusely. She was kept under a doctor's watch and care.

On February 3, 1974, we had our third beautiful daughter in Portage La Prairie, Manitoba. We named her Anita. I was able to see her a day later, when I returned from the North. Kamla told me that she did not notice for almost 11 hours that Anita had her left eye wide open, but the right eye was closed shut. It was not like Kamla to miss something like this. She screamed loudly to make sure the medical staff and nurse heard and came quickly. She showed them that Anita's right eye was closed shut. The doctor was called in quickly and was quite surprised to note that it had somehow been inadvertently left without being cut open. It did not take him long to slit it open very carefully. Anita now was looking at her mom with both of her wide eyes smiling. Anita's first birthday was celebrated in the northern community of Pauingassi, north of Pine Falls. I moved to Thompson in February of 1976.

Kamla was expecting again in 1977. We were in the city, and Kamla had a medical facility to go to as needed. Kamla was visiting a family friend of ours, and I was traveling up north. Kamla was due around this time, and on March 1, 1978, she delivered a baby boy, our fourth child. Our friends, who were watching Kamla in my absence, were very happy that our fourth child was a boy. The nurse at the hospital brought the baby to Kamla after the delivery. We had already named the baby Dileep. When the nurse brought the baby for breastfeeding the second time, Kamla noticed that the baby seemed too big. She immediately called the nurse to check the name. It was not Dileep. Another baby had been picked up by mistake. However, everything turned out to be okay.

We lived in Thompson for nine years. I was no longer teaching, but rather an education administrator with the Department of Indian and Northern Affairs with the Government of Canada. As the children were growing and completing their schooling, we traveled from coast to coast, camping and visiting all of Canada. I also travelled a lot with my work and often asked Kamla to travel with me to conferences and meetings in major cities across Canada.

CHAPTER NINE
Children's Education and Weddings

I am very proud of all of my children and the good lives and education they have been able to have in Canada. The reason I moved to this country was to give my family the best opportunity for a great life, and I feel this was achieved. All of my kids went to university, and they all are married. I have six grandchildren.

Both Kamla and I always emphasized the importance of education with our children. We told our children that if they wanted to pursue a career, they needed to focus on their education. Then they could have the career of their choice. With God's grace, the children heeded our advice.

The thought of arranged marriages was still active in our minds, even after living in Canada for a long time (about 20 years in 1988). By this time, Pinky had turned 21, Minky was 20, Anita was 14, and Dileep was 10 years old. Although it was too early for them to be married, I wanted to be prepared. I started writing to my younger brother and friends and asking them to send names and photos of young suitors that we could look at. Initially, the girls had no idea that I had initiated correspondence in India to find suitable boys for them. Kamla, however, told the girls in my absence about the letters. There was no way the girls would accept this while living in Canada. Their school friends had no idea about arranged marriages. According to them, they would never invite anyone unknown from India to marry them. In fact, they would never go to India to marry someone unknown.

One of the reasons I started planning ahead was that we were the only family from the State of Rajasthan in Winnipeg at that time. Another reason was that the families from other states of India moved around in their own closed communities. To arrange a marriage in those days without your own community was a big challenge for both of us. Later, two more families from Rajasthan moved to Winnipeg but their religion and caste were different than ours. One might wonder why caste and religion would be a concern in Canada. The fact of the matter was that we were still constantly in touch with our families back home in India on a daily basis. Caste and religion is a big concern in our community in India, and any wrong move of ours here in Canada could jeopardize our family's inclusion in our community in India. Any excommunication from the caste or religion in India would have far-reaching effects on all our family members.

My brother placed an advertisement, seeking suitors for our daughters. We decided that once we received replies, my brother's family would go and meet the boys and their families. I also received the bio-data from the boys. I asked my brother to go and meet a boy who claimed to be a doctor. My brother and his wife found out that the boy's claim was false. He was neither a doctor nor studying to be one. He simply wanted to be a doctor once he married my daughter and immigrated to Canada. The boy's parents were also interested in moving to Canada once their son got married to my daughter. We considered this encounter very funny, and we closed that chapter after seeing the boy and his family.

A few days later, we received a letter from the father of another suitor. He wrote that he was very interested in welcoming my daughter as their daughter-in-law. However, he had two daughters, who were of marriage age, and he requested that I find two boys in Canada for them. His son would automatically move to Canada with my daughter after the marriage, and his two daughters would also find homes in Canada once they got married to the boys in Canada. The parents would also move to Canada eventually. Kamla and I found this letter very amusing, and we closed the chapter on this proposal also.

While Kamla was traveling in India with our daughter, Pinky, and our son, Dileep, a friend approached her to say that his son-in-law's younger brother was a bachelor, and he could facilitate a meeting with the boy and his parents. They did not mind having a meeting. They drove to another city to meet the family. The lady of the house greeted them, and she asked a boy to bring tea and snacks for the guests. The boy, who had ruffled hair and was wearing dirty clothing, fetched the snacks. Kamla and Pinky thought that the boy was a servant, as it is quite common for Indian families to have a servant to help with the daily chores. When Kamla asked the lady of the house to see the boy, the lady said, "The boy who served you the tea and snacks is the boy you came here to see." Kamla and Pinky were very disappointed, as they found the boy ill-mannered and illiterate. Therefore, they closed the chapter on this file also.

A friend of mine told me that there was a boy who was a bachelor and came from the same community that I was from. He suggested that I approach him. The boy lived in Portland, USA. This could be our best bet. So I phoned this boy and explained my proposal. The boy replied that he came from a very traditional family and after marrying my daughter he would go back to India. He and his wife would live with his parents. I never phoned him back.

There were a few more proposals, also quite funny and similar in nature. We were building a file of all these letters and decided that we would discuss these proposals with the kids at a later time. In the meantime, the kids had their own plans. They got wind of our plan and told us ahead of any of our discussions that we are wasting our time looking for suitors outside of Canada. We had no choice but to explain to them that we would never go against the wishes of our children. We said that we simply wanted to know what else was available that we could look in to.

One evening, Minky walked in to the house with a young fellow, and she introduced him to us as her boyfriend. We welcomed him in our house, and we spent a good part of the evening with him. After he left the house, we asked Minky how she had met him and why she had chosen him since he was a Tibetan and a Buddhist. Minky said she didn't care about his background. She said, "He had asked me out, and now we both like each other. We want to spend our life together."

Minky with her fiancé Legsang.

We did not bother discussing what we had been planning for them. As time went by, our kids were looking after themselves the way other kids plan their lives in this country. Our kids gave us the impression that we did not need to worry about finding a partner for them. They would not go to India to marry, nor would they have an arranged marriage. All we were allowed to do was to arrange wedding celebrations for them. Their partners and their parents agreed to have the wedding celebrations and ceremonies according to Hindu traditions, along with their own. This was the best compromise, as we did not have any choice in this matter. We enjoyed every wedding over the years.

A year later, we planned the wedding of Minky and Legsang in a downtown hall. The guests praised the ceremony and spoke at the reception about how we were a unique family to have arranged a multicultural marriage. There were two types of wedding ceremonies in the hall – a Hindu wedding ceremony and a Buddhist wedding ceremony.

Minky and Legsang are going through the wedding
rituals with Pinky, Anita, and friends in the background.

During the wedding ceremony of Minky and Legsang, I put on a cassette tape from my younger brother in India. The cassette had a Vedic recital of Hindu traditions, which made everyone emotional. My youngest brother also attended our family's first wedding. He travelled from India only to attend the wedding. He was very happy to see the wedding performed by a Hindu priest according to Hindu traditions. We also noticed that Pinky attended the wedding with her boyfriend from North Bay, who she had met while studying there.

This was the beginning of our family's extension in a multicultural setting.

Pinky graduated from Lake Head University in Thunder Bay, Ontario with a Bachelor of Arts degree in Sociology. She met James Turner there and married him on August 25, 1991. James has a Masters of Education degree. They celebrated their 25th wedding anniversary in 2016. Pinky and Jim live in Winnipeg.

Pinky is with her fiancé Jim.

Pinky and Jim are going through the wedding rituals
in the presence of our friends and relatives.

A married couple: Pinky and Jim share a photograph
with Minky, Legsang, Anita, and Dileep.

Minky graduated from the University of Manitoba with a Bachelor of
Arts degree in Psychology. She is also a Licensed Practical Nurse.

Legsang's family lived in India as many Tibetans had to flee their
country due to a Chinese invasion. Legsang is an IT specialist. Minky
and Legsang married in 1998 and celebrated their 25th wedding
anniversary in August 2014. Together they have four children: Tsering
Asha, Tenzin Raj, Nisha Dolma, and Ajai Renzin. All four children are
in university. Tsering Asha celebrated her wedding to Dara Eshaghian
in July 2015. She also graduated from the University of Calgary with
a Bachelor of Arts degree in Political Science and is looking to pursue
a career in law.

Anita graduated from the University of Manitoba with a Bachelor of
Arts degree in Political Science and then completed her Masters degree
in Political Science and Public Administration from the University of
Winnipeg in 1999. She married Lindsay Sutherland in 2001. Lindsay
was a teacher by profession but changed his career to be an IT specialist.

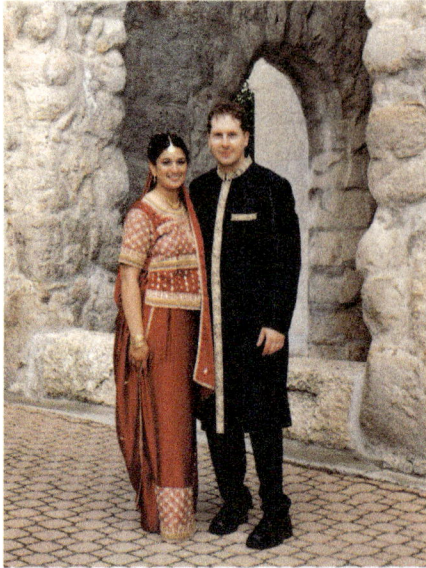

Anita with her fiancé Lindsay.

Anita and Lindsay are going through the wedding rituals at an altar.

Anita and Lindsay have two boys: Anil Dev and Shawn Jai.

Dileep graduated from the University of Manitoba with a Bachelor of Agro-business Science Degree. Dileep married Elizabeth Cecil from Hastings, Nebraska in 2006 at a civil court in Tennessey, USA. On August 17, 2007 we performed a Hindu wedding ceremony for them.

Dileep with his fiancée Elizabeth.

Dileep and Elizabeth are going through the wedding rituals.

Liz's parents and family members came to Winnipeg from Nebraska to attend the wedding ceremony, which they enjoyed immensely. Liz recently completed her PhD in Asian Studies from the prestigious Brown University in Providence, Rhode Island. Liz travels to India frequently for her research and can speak Hindi, which I find very impressive.

In July 2015, my wife, all of my children, their spouses, and my grandchildren were in Calgary, Alberta for the wedding of my granddaughter Tsering Asha Leba with Dara Eshaghian, from London, Ontario. It was a joyous occasion and the first time all of us had been together in one location in about seven years. I was fortunate to also celebrate my 75th birthday.

CHAPTER TEN
Memorable Stories

Anita's Sickness and Family Services in Winnipeg

We went to India when Anita was only one year old. It had been five years since we had been there. Everyone in the family was anxiously waiting to see us and greeted us with garlands when we arrived at the airport.

We had one suitcase full of Enfalac baby formula (powdered milk) for Anita. We were a family of five traveling to India, and we had ten big suitcases, each weighing seventy pounds, and ten carry-on bags. It was a nightmare for us trying to handle all of that baggage. However, with the help of an airport porter, we managed to get out of the airport terminal.

There were plenty of gift items for every member of the family and friends. After the first day of our stay, all our suitcases were empty as we had distributed all the gifts. Although we would be in India for eight weeks, we had taken almost forty containers of Enfalac baby formula for Anita – just in case.

Anita, being a one-year-old cute baby, was everyone's darling. After a couple of days, Anita started to get sick. The Canadian baby formula was not working for her. We had to resort to a famous Indian formula from Amul dairies under the doctor's advice. Several days passed by, and the Enfalac baby formula was of no use for Anita.

My younger brother, who was a medical student at that time, found some use for the Enfalac. Since it was full of essential vitamins and minerals, he started drinking it himself. He said he was feeling healthier because of all its strengthening ingredients. He would drink it two or three times a day just like a baby. Anita, however, was getting weaker by the day, and it got to the point that we had to leave India in a panic. Anita started getting dehydrated. We had to call the doctor in our hotel room in Bombay (now called Mumbai).

We reached the hospital in Winnipeg without delay for Anita's treatment. Once Anita was hospitalized, she spent three or four days while her body fully recovered hydration.

The doctor even made a comment that we were lucky to bring her to the hospital when we did. We were at the hospital day and night with Anita, but one day we decided to take a break and go to a movie after our visit.

Pinky and Minky were at home under the care of our close friend. We asked our friend to feed the girls lunch, as we might be late coming home. My friend went to buy lunch for the girls at ten after twelve. My friend was a bit late coming home with the food. Pinky was only eight years old. She had the hospital phone number in Anita's wardroom. She just wanted to talk to us, so she phoned the hospital number.

The attending nurse picked up the phone, and told Pinky that we had already left the hospital after visiting Anita. The nurse also happened to enquire why our elder daughter was phoning at this hour. It prompted her to ask Pinky if she had eaten. Pinky told the nurse that she and her sister hadn't had lunch. Pinky did not tell the nurse that my friend had gone to pick up food for them. The children usually answer in short sentences and won't say more than what is asked. The nurse thought that my two daughters were alone at home and hungry, and that there was no one to look after them.

We returned home at four o'clock after the movie was over. To my surprise, my friend was sitting with the girls, and a supervisor from the childcare agency was interviewing them. The officer had a report prepared against us saying that we were neglecting our daughters and not feeding them.

My friend explained the situation and that he had only gone next door to a restaurant to get food for them. The officer also interviewed me as well. I clarified the situation, but for the next 3 months, the officer visited us to make sure everything was ok. We still to this day laugh about the incident, and we made sure to tell the story at Anita and Lindsay's wedding.

Dileep's Birth and an Incident During Our Indian Visit

Our son Dileep was born on March 1, 1978 in Thompson. We had a great celebration at our home. My mother also had a very big celebration back home in India as soon she heard the news of her grandson's birth in Canada. She distributed sweets to everyone in our village. She organized singing and dancing parties to celebrate the event. We did the same thing in Thompson by inviting our friends.

Our house was filled with joy, good wishes, congratulations, and friends. Good wishes also started pouring in from India by phone and in congratulatory cards. Both Kamla's and my parents started calling us to go to India with the baby. They could not wait to see him. We had to make plans to travel to India as soon as we could. We were advised to wait until the baby was at least two year's old.

We planned our trip to India after two years. Two days after we had arrived, we saw a group of eunuchs in front of our house with drums and music. Everyone in the group was dancing and singing louder and louder, drawing everyone's attention in the neighborhood including ours. I was told that the eunuchs in India have a powerful communication network, and they very quickly find out about a newborn baby boy.

They go to the family and give good wishes to the baby and the parents. In return they charge a fee. It is compulsory that they hold the baby boy in their arms, and that they check to make sure the baby is a male offspring. If the baby is of a female sex, they happily return the baby to the parents without demanding anything from the parents. If the baby is of neither sex, then it is a eunuch, and the baby has to go. They take the baby and look after it until it grows up and joins the group to perform eunuchs' rites. This is the story I was told.

Even the social system of the country is unable to free the baby from their hands. If it is a baby boy, they will not return the baby to the parents until they recover their fixed charges. It was about 5000 rupees, plus some clothing and jewelry at that time. The parents can give more if they wish. I hear that now their charges have gone up to 21,000 rupees.

Anita was six years old, and she was also with us. When she saw her brother being held up by the eunuchs, she cried profusely and demanded her little brother back from them. There was no room for negotiations. The onlookers from the neighborhood were enjoying the show, which was nothing new to them. I was given an assurance by the family that our baby was safe with them. It is considered a good omen in the country if the group of eunuchs dances with the baby boy in their arms. I gave a little more than what was expected, and Dileep was given back to us. Anita was happy to see her baby brother back in our arms. I kept thinking about this custom, which is not even known in the West. We still talk about it.

Dileep's Haircut in India

We had haircut ceremony for our son Dileep in Canada. The custom requires that the original hair of the baby boy needs to be shaved between the age of two and three years. In India, you do this ceremony in front of the deity Hanuman in a temple. The family and friends gather around, and the barber shaves the baby's hair in a ritualistic manner. The hair is then offered to the deity Hanuman in a gesture that all egos are surrendered, so the baby will grow with humility and with his blessings.

We brought the hair and offered it to the deity Hanuman at the famous Hanuman temple, which is only 60 kilometers from our place. Balaji is the deity Hanuman. He is an immortal devotee of Lord Rama.

Lord Rama was in exile for fourteen years. Lord Rama's consort Sita was abducted by the demon Ravana of Sri Lanka. It was deity Hanuman who helped Lord Rama to bring back Sita from house arrest from Sri Lanka after Rama killed the demon king Ravana. Deity Hanuman, with the help of his army of monkeys, built the bridge in the ocean from the southern tip of India to Sri Lanka, so that the battle with the demon king Ravana could be won. The bridge is known as Rama-Setu and is still visible from the air.

Hanuman Temple and Patients

The Balaji temple is situated in a town called Mehndipur, which is about eighty kilometers from the city of Jaipur. The presiding deity Hanuman is known to give instant blessings to any devotees who faithfully go there to pray. It is also believed that mental illness due to mythical possession by ghosts or schizophrenia is cured in that temple. People from all around the country and abroad go to this particular temple for blessings.

There are two huge corridors in front of the temple. These corridors are filled with mental patients, who people believe are possessed by ghosts or supernatural spirits. These patients need to be cured. It is believed that only Hanuman can rid them of the evil spirits. Rich people donate millions of Indian rupees to the temple to ensure the treatment reaches their family members, who go to this temple. These patients sit all day, and swing their long hair violently. They also use sticks to bang their head and bodies while swinging their hair. The sight can be scary to some. This happened to Pinky, Minky, Anita, and Dileep. The kids found the sight horrifying to them, and they decided to run away from there. I assured the kids that there was no need to be scared, as we were in the midst of thousands of pilgrims. Mehndipur Balaji is now a bustling city of hotels and shops for tourists and devotees alike.

We had a big feast in a motel hall after the hair cut ceremony was over. Family and friends showered Dileep with blessings and gifts. It was a very big event in our family, and everyone present enjoyed it immensely. We had all the celebrations for Dileep except passing him through and under Krishna's altar, as we had to return to Canada before *Krishna Janmasthmi* (the birth date of Divine Krishna), and we didn't have any divine processions of Krishna where we lived.

We named him Dileep because Dileep was a king in India with a good heart, and he was well received in his kingdom for his good deeds for the welfare of his subjects. He had the divine blessings of Lord Krishna. This name, we felt, fit well for our son, as naming a child should carry some meaning according to our culture and traditions.

Kamla's Childhood Secrets

When my grandfather decided that I must get married, he invited a couple of our relatives, the family priest, the family barber, and the attendant to discuss the plan to look for a suitable girl for me. The people informed him that he should go to the village of Merera near the town of Todabhim to see a girl there. My grandfather decided to go along with another person. He arrived at the door of Kamla's family.

Kamla was wandering in from primary school and came inside the house without noticing my grandfather with another person. My grandfather had already decided that Kamla was the girl for me. He told me a couple of things later. "I have seen this girl," he said. Her name is Kamla. She has a very fair complexion, and she will fit with you in every situation. Though she is a cowgirl, she will be a suitable partner at every occasion. You will be very happy with Kamla in your life. Kamla will also bring good luck to you. I have had her horoscope checked by our priest. You do not need to worry about seeing her, as I assure you of what I have just stated."

He also told me another story that Kamla's father told him when he was visiting their house. Kamla was only two years old in 1947. India was in the midst of independence from Britain and a partition with Pakistan. The town of Todabhim had a concentration of Muslims. There were bands of Muslim youths and other ages looking for communal riots in the area. They wanted to get into some of the action, as there were all kinds of horrifying fights between Hindus and Muslims at the time of the partition.

Hindu youths were also roaming around in the towns and villages for the same purpose. Kamla's family had a few goats. There was a kid among them. When a group of Muslim youths passed through their street, parents took little babies inside their houses and hid them in the rooms. However, somehow baby Kamla had been left outside in a hurry after they had locked the main gate of their house.

When her parents realized that Kamla was in the small crib outside, her mother rushed outside and put a big basket over her and the kid to hide them from the hoodlums. It was a normal practice for families who own goats to have a big basket handy to cover the kids, so that they would not run away from the yard.

The baskets are very well ventilated. The bottom is covered with a cloth and turned upside down to make it look like a covered umbrella. They put something heavy like a stone on top, so that the kid does not run away with the basket. Now the basket had a kid and the baby together inside, all covered up. Kamla extended her hand outside the crib. Somehow she grabbed the kid's ear. A baby's grip is usually quite powerful and tight. She would not let the kid go. Her grip was hurting the kid, and it started screaming "main-main-main-main," as goats do. The kid's scream drew the attention of the band of Muslims. They stopped by the house and shouted at her father that he should keep his kid under control or they would take it away. Then they walked away. Kamla saved herself! She told me this story over a cup of coffee.

The Hard Time Kamla Had in India in My Absence

Everyone in the family was feeling excited to see me go abroad. The family members were happy that I was going to build a better future, not only for myself, but also for the whole family. I was my parents' eldest son. My parents had high hopes for me. My grandfather, however, had mixed feelings about my departure. He was not sure if it was a good idea for me to leave my young wife with two daughters behind.

Pinky was only 16 months old, and Minky had been born only two days prior to my departure. We did not even have enough time to properly name Minky. We just matched the name with Pinky. I was busy packing and making travel arrangements, while Kamla was in labour in the hospital.

We also packed our furniture and household goods to go with Kamla, as she would be living with my parents in our home in the village.

Minky sent a funny e-mail when I was celebrating my 41-year anniversary of my arrival in Canada on September 9, 2009. Minky's birthday falls on September 5. She wrote:

> I was born on a hot summer day in Jaipur, India on September 5, 1968 at Jaipur General Hospital. My older sister Pinky was trying on her new red jacket that Mommy had bought her from the local school and shouting out funny sounds, R-D-P-C. My mommy looked down at me pleasingly and said, "Another beautiful baby girl, Nityaji, what beautiful name shall we give her?" All of a sudden, Pinky looked up from her game and said to my beaming parents, "Eh! What is her name? Could it be as beautiful as mine?" Of course it will be, said my young innocent mother.
>
> Suddenly, Papa remembered he had a flight to catch. He was going half way around the world to the new world called Kanaada. (That's what Mommy called it)!

Mommy was upset, but understood the sacrifices that were being made for the good of the family, and she said in her bellowing, excited voice, "Yes, Nityaji, you better leave at once. Don't worry about us, I will take care of the girls!" Papa then pulled out his wallet and offered Mommy the last of his rupees (he would find out later he would do alright in Kanaada) and said, "Is this enough?" Mommy said, "No, but I will take it and make sure you have lots more when I come to Kanaada with the girls. I have heard many great things about Kanaada, and I can't wait to live there... I will have lots of friends, parties, clothes...blah...blah."

Papa was just about to leave the hospital room, when the ward nurse walked in and said, "Hey, mister, is *ka naam kya hey* (meaning, what name are you going to give her)?" Unable to come up with anything while under this great pressure, all he could say was "Minky". Pinky stopped shouting and couldn't understand why papa was calling her something different and Mommy was too excited to notice, as she was dreaming about Kanaada. Then the nurse, who couldn't understand what was happening and why this man was leaving his wife and two beautiful girls in such a hurry (and on top of that his one daughter was named Pinky and now the other one was Minky!), could only say with confusion, "*Achha* (okay), your new baby is Minky!"

Happy Canada Arrival Day, Papa!! That's how I imagine I got my name...ha...ha!!

Kamla had a week to pick up her stuff and leave for the village with my parents and two little girls to live without me for at least two years. I had a plan to spend one year at the university and then one year working in Canada. If I decided to stay beyond two years, then I would seek permanent residency and sponsor Kamla and my two girls to join me.

If I decided to go back to India after my two-year assignment, then everything would be back to where I left it. I sincerely followed my plan of action and completed my two years as intended. However, the second year was full of uncertainty. To go back or to seek permanent residency was a big question and a big decision. My teaching experience might not be of any use back home because the curriculum and teaching methodology were completely different, and there was no possibility of adapting to the Western way of teaching so quickly. I had to apply for permanent residency soon to allow time for sponsoring the family so that Kamla and the kids could join me without any delays.

Back in India, Kamla was under a lot of pressure from both sides of our family. Members of the family were commenting on her living alone in India, while I was abroad alone. Most of the comments were negative in nature. People were making remarks to her that I might not go back to India and might not bring her and the girls to Canada. They told her that I might be indulging in some affair with another woman in Canada. People were commenting that I had a girlfriend that wanted to marry me. Some were commenting that if I could leave my girlfriend behind, then I could decide to leave my wife behind too. Some were saying that Kamla would find a tough life in India if I did not attend to her soon.

Some old women from the neighborhood were making comments that I left her behind because Kamla had two girls. I am the eldest son in the family, and all my new family had was two girls. They said, "He will never come back to India to live. He will not come back for his family. Most of the people who have gone to a Western country never return. The majority of them marry another woman and settle down there. Some of them send a little bit of money and keep promising to their wives they will come back and that she will not be left alone." Most of the comments directed against her were of no value.

Kamla did not pay attention to any of these negative comments. She had full confidence in what we had decided before I left, and in this hope she kept on waiting for the right time. My friend was very helpful to her for arranging her travel documents, and when the time came, she was ready to depart to join me. I applied for permanent residency in order to sponsor Kamla and the girls to settle in Canada. I never regretted my decision for the future of my family. I successfully sponsored Kamla, Pinky, and Minky after two years, and they safely arrived to join me.

Kamla told me that she had to go through some hard times during the time I was away from them. However, the sad memories faded very quickly the moment they boarded their westbound plane to Canada. They felt the same as I had felt when I had boarded my flight two years earlier. There was a sense of excitement about restarting our family life in a new country. They did not care for the hardships they had to go through in my absence. They lived in hope, and nothing else mattered to them. Kamla's prime concern was the proper upbringing of Pinky and Minky in my absence at my parents' and at her parent's homes. She made sure that both daughters did not feel deprived of anything and that they were happy and healthy.

She kept herself focused without any hesitation, and that kept her hopes alive. She knew that she would be going to Canada within two years, and there were no two ways about it. I was waiting for their arrival at the airport's arrival terminal. Kamla was looking all around the airport while holding Pinky and Minky, as well as carry-on bags. She saw me from the glass doors and immediately nudged Pinky and Minky to see me from upstairs. I grabbed both of the girls first to receive them, and then the bags, as soon as they arrived inside the terminal. I hugged them all. Kamla had completed her journey successfully, and I had whisked them away to our new home.

New World

We had three bedrooms in our house. I put one suitcase in one bedroom for Pinky and another suitcase for Minky in the second bedroom. I put two other suitcases in the master bedroom. Pinky was curiously looking at my placing the suitcases in three different rooms. Minky did not pay any attention at this time, as she was holding on to her mother. I did not pay much attention either. However, I realized later that the girls were not used to having their own rooms. Kamla knew already that we were going to live in a bungalow with three bedrooms, as I had told her before they even arrived.

Pinky sat down on the bed in her room and looked around. There was only one picture on the wall. I had received this picture from Air India when I first arrived. The other pictures were of Pinky's baby photograph and a photograph of our family members, which had been taken at the airport when I left. Pinky kept looking at the pictures, bed covers, pillows, and other articles in the room. She did not bother looking at her own suitcase at this time.

We wanted to eat our supper first, but Pinky, being tired, fell asleep on her bed. Kamla was busy in another room showing Minky her doll that I had bought for her, as well as her room for her to sleep in. I had bought some sandwiches for supper on our way home from the airport. After sometime we woke Pinky up to have supper with us.

Pinky and Minky ate their sandwiches without any fuss, but Kamla was not happy to see sandwiches for supper, though she knew what sandwiches were before she arrived in Canada. She decided she wanted to cook something spicy in the kitchen. So she looked for spices in the cupboards, but none were to be found. I had never bought spices while living on my own. I only had some cookies in a jar, some cereal boxes, milk, bread, oranges, and apple juice in the kitchen. This would all change now that Kamla was here.

It was Saturday morning, and I took Kamla and the girls grocery shopping. We entered the Safeway store, where she could buy anything she needed. Kamla was used to buying fresh vegetables and fruits from street vendors, flour from the mill using her own container, wheat or barley or sugar by weight in an open bag, and other household items from different shops in a market in India. She was very surprised to see a wide variety of shops and items under one roof in a single shopping centre. She picked up a few vegetables, a bag of flour, a bag of sugar, a jug of milk, a pound of butter, and a loaf of bread.

Unfortunately, she did not find the spices of her choice. She picked up salt and pepper, ground ginger (fresh ginger was nowhere to be seen in those days), cloves, nutmeg (even though she did not know how to use it), a bag of onions, a bag of potatoes, a five-pound bag of Uncle Ben's rice, and a few other items that she felt would be interesting and useful.

Kamla did not see anyone from India or from another country while shopping at the mall. She could only converse with me during our shopping trip. We did not buy anything for the girls at this time, as we planned another trip to the city for more shopping, and that would be for clothing, electronics, and toys for the girls. Kamla prepared her first Indian meal in Canada consisting of mixed peas and potatoes, a plain bowl of boiled rice, flour *halva* (a sweet dish of flour, milk, sugar, and water), *chapattis* (puffed bread), and milk. It was a meal of both aesthetic and authentic taste! It was the beginning of many amazing meals that Kamla would not only cook for us but for thousands of people as she mastered her culinary talent.

We enquired about an Indian-owned grocery store in the city, and we went there. Kamla started grabbing large quantities of each spice available in the store and various other items of Indian grocery. However, before she could get to the checkout, the storekeeper interrupted her, saying that she would not be able to purchase such a large quantity of spices, rice, flour, and fresh Indian vegetables at one time. He mentioned that the store only received a limited quantity of these items, and there were a few Indian families in the city who also needed the same items.

Due to the limited quantities of these items, he had to ration each family. Kamla was a little disappointed but understood and allowed the storekeeper to package the items she needed according to his rationing system.

While the keeper was busy packaging, Kamla enquired about the other Indian families residing in the city, so that she could develop some social contacts. She was happy to get a list of a few families to contact so that she could start building communication by phone. She brought the items she needed, although in very little quantities that she never expected. She laughs to this day that she was only able to buy five green peppers, fifteen cloves, and four ounces of ground spices from India.

The first shopping trip was a great success, even though the groceries were limited, but for the list of some Indian families. It was getting late in the evening, and I had to drive about 100 kilometers out of town. Our next outing would be a few days later. This would allow Kamla and the girls to get settled in the house and explore their new surroundings.

CHAPTER ELEVEN
Life in Canada with Ongoing Communication with India

After leaving India, we started getting letters from family and friends. Most of the letters had contents packed with emotions, as expected. Both sides of our family felt our absence immediately after we left. My grandfather already told me at the time of bidding farewell that we might or might not meet again. He did not believe that I had left India never to return, and that I would have my family in the faraway country of Canada.

My brothers wrote to me that their lives seemed to be shattered forever, as they could not comprehend the fact that we would not be living in India anymore. Everyone in the family was sending messages for us to visit India as soon as possible, although we had just arrived in Canada. The family members were eager to hear our voices. I had to write them a letter with an exact date and time of when we would make a phone call to them. Later, I would book this call with the phone company.

My letter would reach well in advance of my phone call. Before I moved into my house with Kamla and the girls, my phone was on a party line system. There were three party rings on the same phone. I knew my ring tone, so that I could pick up the call. The other two parties would also know when I was talking on the phone. My close friend had a phone in India. I had to book his telephone number to speak to my family members.

My mother, father, brothers, and sister, along with Kamla's whole family, would congregate at my friend's home on the day of my phone call. At the appointed time, the telephone operator would connect my phone to Montreal then to Vancouver then to Sydney (Australia) then to Bombay, and then to Jaipur city at my friend's phone line. All this happened through the ocean cable system.

I was told that everyone present in the room used to cheer as soon the phone rang! If the phone line was poor at the other end, then we sat on the phone waiting, sometimes for hours. My friend's family and our families were getting to know each other quite well through this process.

My friend was getting used to hosting lunches and dinners for all these people using the party line phone. Sometimes our phone conversations did not materialize for hours. When we were connected, the sound was usually very poor. Most of the time, we were just saying "Hello." Sadly, I was charged about $4.00 a minute, just because the line was connected. I had to negotiate with the phone company to settle the bill, even if we never had a proper conversation.

Our family members often returned home disappointed without having had a conversation with us. But that was the nature of international calls during the early sixties and seventies. We were mostly writing letters for a number of years and booking phone calls once in a while in between. We were also making trips to India every three to four years to visit family and friends. Our family members used to send a list of items that we were supposed to take back with us every time we visited India. We enjoyed taking gifts to every family member and to our friends from Canada. They loved the gift items from Canada.

As soon we arrived from India, we used to be busy collecting gift items all over again for our next trip. We were also getting a lot of gift items from India, along with the purchased items of our own. Most of my earnings were spent traveling to India, sending money to my brothers and parents in India, buying gift items for families, and meeting living expenses at home in Canada. I did not pay much attention to a savings plan or to financial planning for the future of my own family. After my children got married, and after my retirement, I found out that financial planning is of the utmost priority for every family living in the West. For some people like myself, it is often too late.

Unfortunately, this is the case for a majority of immigrant families living in Western countries. Fortunately or unfortunately, the demand for gift items and financial assistance to our families back home never stops.

We kept getting letters for almost twenty years until telephone service became cheaper and more accessible in late 1990s. My brothers would write that it was getting difficult for them to concentrate on any kind of work, as they felt our absence. Two of my brothers found jobs through the assistance of my relatives. One of my brothers left his job and started his own business. He struggled to establish his business to the point that he used to have nightmares even in daytime. Sometimes he would see a ghost in a bird perched by the window of the house he was renting. Another brother would find himself in financial problems to the point that he will steal old silver coins, gold, and jewelry from the house to sell. One brother left home for job training without making any financial arrangements.

My parents were not rich and were not able to meet their demands. I would reach out and try to provide whatever financial assistance I was able to arrange at that time. They would write to me that one of our family members was possessed by a ghost, and that her parents were running around with her to the local medicine men to rid her of the devil. This was simply false news and made up to get my attention so I would not forget the family in India. Someone would write to me that our family needed a Massey Ferguson tractor for agricultural purposes, and that I was in a position to book it by depositing money in advance in Canadian dollars so we could take a quick delivery ahead of everyone else.

All would be arranged, but when the tractor arrived, no one was prepared to take the delivery due to the unavailability of funds. I was not prepared to purchase such a big item from my own pocket. I do not know what happened to this transaction later and usually was never told about all of the money I provided them with.

My brother would write to me that he wanted to buy a house, a motorcycle, and a shop. He was in dire need of money to finance his projects. I bought him the motorcycle, but declined his other demands. Later he would write that I should send him a ticket to come visit Canada. I bought him a return ticket and arranged his visit.

Everyone would constantly write to me to bring them a camera, a good supply of the latest fashionable ties, shirts, suits, electronic transistors, record players, tape recorders, fashionable silk saris from Japan, winter clothing for the little kids, leather shoes, the latest wrist watches, movie cameras, sun glasses, small pots and pans and appliances, Johnny Walker Black Label Scotch, and above all, a draft in Canadian dollars!

After all, they also wanted to show off in their social circle that their eldest brother was living in North America, a land of milk and honey. I also received career resumes from a number of my friends, relatives, and some family members. Everyone wrote that they were fed up living in India, and that they wanted to leave. They wanted to come to Canada. Some wanted to open up a business in India, and I was requested to send some seed money for their business, as well as some foreign-made tools and equipment. The demands of this nature were proving meaningless to me from a practical perspective being so far away. This was also causing too much distraction for me in moving ahead in my career and my own professional development.

I do not know how I was able to satisfy everyone's demands, but I tried my best to send some things and bring some items by packing big and heavy suitcases every time we went to India. Looking at the social needs, I sponsored two of my friends, two of my brothers, one of Kamla's cousins, and one of my nephews to visit us, to take a tour of Canada, and to attend our children's wedding ceremonies at various times between 1975 to 2001.

I do not know how I did it, but I did it out of passion and love for our family and friends. Unfortunately, everything has changed. Whatever was done has so far turned out to be futile. Maybe I did not do enough, but after my retirement, I tightened up my belt, as I had no choice. I declined to sponsor and fund the university education in Canada of one of my nephews.

My younger brothers jointly said in front of all our relatives, friends, and family members that we have not done anything for them, and that they came to Canada out of their own good fortune. They said we were desperate to invite them and have them attend our daughters' weddings. It was not a favor to them. I guess, once you stop a trend, feelings run high against you. I am now an outsider as well as a foreign national in their eyes. My mother told me that I should not offer money to anyone, because once you offer money to one, there would be hundreds more in line from family to friends. I would never be able to meet everyone's demands. Sending money would only make family members indifferent for not doing anything. This was the most valuable advice I received from my mother.

It seems as though the world has taken a turn for the worse. My children and the future generation may loose a connection with the new generation. Both sides of family members need to be interested in maintaining a relationship. We, however, were treated very well when we offered financial gifts! We were treated with utmost honor in social get-togethers. We now feel that this type of treatment is only temporary. But I am going to leave it the way it is, as I do not have the energy or time to spare for sorting out this type of futile social tangle. I ponder upon the nice letters filled with love and respect that I used to receive. It is now just another chapter of a family history.

Observing Festivals and Holidays

I do not only remember celebrating New Year's Eve throughout the years, as there were many holidays celebrated throughout India every month!

Government buildings and the buildings of various social institutions were lit up to celebrate the New Year. People bought all sorts of items in the market. Schools and colleges organized drama and cultural evenings filled with dancing and singing competitions. The country observes this as a national holiday. Everyone feels good with high hopes and new dreams to fulfill.

The Indian Republic Day falls on January 26, which is also observed as a National holiday. Mahatma Gandhi Jayanti is also a national holiday. August 15 is India's Independence Day, which is celebrated with great pomp and show. There are a number of religious festivals that belong to different religious groups, and that are celebrated by a majority of Indians. These festivals are Holi, Diwali, Idul Fitter, Ramadan, Guru Nanak Jayanti, Christmas, Baisakhi, Mahavir Jayanti, Swaminarayan Jayanti, Pongal, Maha Shiva Ratri, Krishna Janmasthmi, and Ram Navmi, to name a few. These holidays are also observed as national holidays. In Canada, the schools are closed for two summer months in July and August. There are a few civic holidays as well. India enjoys observing one or two national holidays every month.

As soon I came to Canada, these Indian holidays simply disappeared for me in 1968. First of all, I did not see many families from India, and secondly, I got busy in my own field of work as a new immigrant. People held a few gatherings with a few Indian families in their own homes and individually observed these festivities on a very small scale. As the population of the people of Indian origin grew, all these festivals became observed colorfully and on a large scale with great participation along with the mainstream population.

I arrived in September, and I quickly found out that we observe and celebrate in Canada a number of national holidays as well. There are two or more national, religious, and civic holidays that people of Canada observe and celebrate almost every month. The main holidays are New Year's Day, Valentine's Day, Good Friday, Easter Sunday, Easter Monday, Mother's Day, Victoria Day, Father's Day, Canada Day, Labour Day, Thanksgiving Day, Remembrance Day, Christmas Day, Boxing Day, and New Year's Eve, to name a few.

I found so much similarity in observing, and celebrating some of these holidays. Christmas is to celebrate the birth of Jesus Christ. *Diwali* is to celebrate the arrival of Lord Rama (an incarnation of God Vishnu). *Krishna Janmasthmi* is to celebrate the birth of Lord Krishna (an incarnation of God Vishnu in a different age). These are celebrated as a festival of lights, signifying the light over darkness and the victory of good over evil. *Ramadan* and *Id* also signify the power of good over evil. People light up homes, streets, public buildings, and exchange gifts among families and friends, along with enjoying feasts and big parties. Canada Day in Canada and Independence Day (August 15) in India signify the independence from colonialism. New Year's Day is universally celebrated to observe new hope and a positive forward outlook.

I did not see families observing Brother's Day here in Canada, which is observed in India and known as *Rakhshabandhan*, during which a sister ties a thread on her brother's wrist as a promise by the brother that he will protect his sister in times of need. However, we observe Father's Day and Mother's Day in Canada. Nowadays these are observed all over the world. Young people are now observing Valentine's Day in India in spite of fierce opposition from a large number of fanatic religious and cultural die-hards.

CHAPTER TWELVE
Exploring Canada To See Her Beauty

I decided to travel in Canada from the East Coast to the West Coast. The children were young and eager to see the country. I bought an executive recreation van, which had a beautiful interior with big sliding screen windows and facilities like a convertible sofa to bed for four people. It also had a water cooler, built-in propane heater-stove, a small closet in the back, attractive dome lights, a round coffee table, revolving seats, and a small television cum radio. Tenting gear for camping could also be attached on the side of the van. Kamla and I decided to take road trips by staying in KOA campgrounds and enjoying the outdoors at the same time.

We decided to travel to the East in one summer and to the West another summer for two reasons: One being that the country is so big, and it is impossible to cover all the beautiful attractions in one single trip. Secondly, my van in the early 80s became so popular that one fellow in the North bought it and paid more money than what I bought it for. This I found interesting, as new vehicles depreciate very fast, and here I was getting almost $5000 more after driving it all summer for camping. We completed our tour of Canada, which was most enjoyable and memorable.

Kamla and I are keeping our recreation van ready for the tour.

I am trying to show my love for Canada through my pictures that I snapped during the travel, as the country looks beautiful through pictures.

I found this country most fascinating. Besides living and enjoying every day of life, I became interested in taking pictures of the sites that interested me. I had never seen snow before I came to Canada. I was fascinated with the vast and open wilderness. I marveled to find the largest landmass between the Pacific Ocean in the West and the Atlantic Ocean in the East. Canada also has five and half time zones, which I found very inconvenient while traveling from the East Coast to the West Coast. Not only that, the times change twice a year, and people have to adjust watches and clocks in the fall and spring.

I found the people friendly and inviting.

Canada's natural beauty is quite captivating, as there are snow-capped rocky mountain peaks in the West; flat prairies in the centre; the Appalachian Mountain Range in the East; and a picturesque South and a snowy Arctic Ocean in the North. There are roads everywhere, and driving on divided highways is mostly fun-filled.

My Canada pictures show things and places I visited.

I got busy in my studies as soon as I arrived at the university.

Here is my study room, where I spent majority of my time studying.

I am enjoying the sight of a vast open frozen lake.

A lake with open waters along the community.

Here are fellow teachers enjoying outdoors.

Boating is fun in Cross Lake.

Standing alone in the wilderness

A snowy road for Bombardiers and skidoos

A beautiful lake and spruce trees

Once my family joined me, we had more pictures, as we widely travelled.

Outdoors in the afternoon

Pinky and Minky enjoying the outdoors

Kamla and Minky enjoying the outdoors

We are enjoying the outdoors with our friends.

Beautiful falls

Quebec's National Assembly

Scenic Quebec City

Beautiful wall murals in Quebec City.

Bridge outside Quebec City

Hikers relaxing on a hill at Banff National Park

Kamla is ready for a Gondola ride in Banff National Park.

Kamla is riding a horse at Banff National Park.

Nityanand and Kamla enjoying a horse ride in Banff National Park

Dad is helping Dileep to pick fruits in the Okanagan Valley.

Pishew falls near Thompson, Manitoba.

The water fountain is providing a cool breeze.

Royal Canadian Mint in Winnipeg City

Enjoying the lakeside

Riding my motorcycle in Thompson

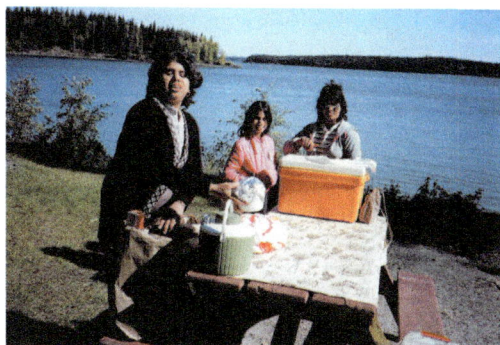

A picnic at Paint Lake near Thompson, Manitoba

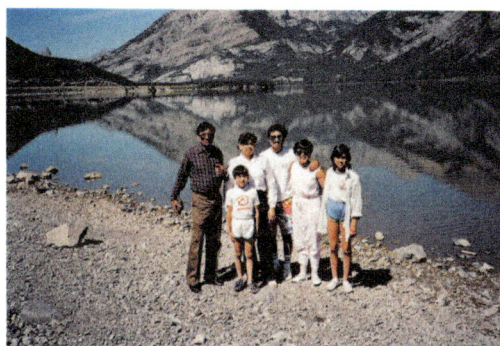

With friends in Alberta, Canada

A gondola ride to Grouse Mountain, B.C.

Mountain goats

Dileep posing in Edmonton Mall

The kids enjoying water slides in Edmonton Mall

Anita trying a golf game

We reached the hilltop restaurant by gondola in Banff National Park.

A panoramic view of the mountains

Beautiful Lake Louise

A great view of Lake Louise

Walking around at Lake Louise

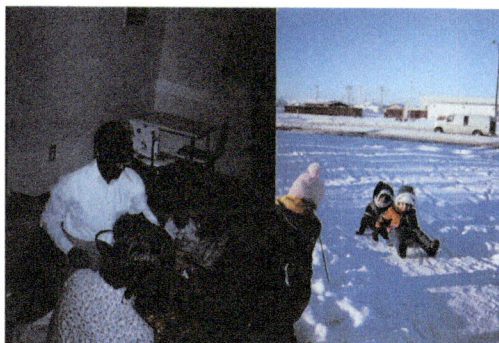

The kids are enjoying a sled ride.

Pedal boats

Having great fun riding pedal boats

Bouchart gardens in Vancouver, B.C.

Nice flower beds

Enticing walkabouts

Mesmerizing gardens

We are enjoying the lakeside and beach.

Resting in the woods

A view of downtown Toronto from the hotel room and Quebec.

A view of Quebec City

A view of Vancouver

Thompson City covered in the snow

Our basement in Thompson

A winter carnival with snow sculptures in Thompson.

Kamla, Dileep, and Anita are enjoying the winter carnival of snow sculptures in Winnipeg, Manitoba.

Most of our travel in Canada was done in the early 80s, when we were living in Thompson, Manitoba. We travelled some more places after moving to Winnipeg in 1985.

We enjoyed traveling in Canada more, as I was driving my recreational van with the whole family, which provided total freedom for all of us. We drove as much distance as I could cover, and we stopped wherever we found nearby KOA campgrounds.

It was fun to travel. We still travel by van, but this time there are only two of us, as the grandchildren travel with their parents. I find travel by my own vehicle more convenient and enjoyable. There are no restrictions in packing our suitcases, hauling stuff with us, and stopping overnight wherever we find it convenient.

Canada sure is a beautiful country.

CHAPTER THIRTEEN
A Learning Environment

My Grandfather used to tell me stories about good and evil people and situations. He taught me that every one of us is born with two sets of treasure chests. The first chest contains virtues. Based on what I heard from him, I can list some of them below:

> Love, Kindness, Humility, Nonviolence, Sacrifice,
>
> Dutifulness, Honesty, Morality, Gentleness,
>
> Regard for life, Good Deeds, Salvation,
>
> Desire to make people's life better, Courage, Patience, Civility,
>
> Living within moral boundaries, Pardonable heart,
>
> Devotion to the divine, Welcoming, and
>
> Progressive thinking.

The second chest contains the evil called vices as below:

> Lust, Anger, Arrogance, Greed, Cruelty,
>
> Destructive feelings, Violence, Sinfulness, Demonic urges,
>
> Jealousy, Hate, Vengefulness, Enmity, Con Artistry,
>
> Manipulative nature, and Cruelty.

He told me that the main source of virtues are love and kindness, while the root cause of vices is anger. He also advised me that I should find time to read about these characteristics whenever I could during my lifetime, and that I should practice using the treasure of virtues, while I should practice controlling the treasure chest of vices or even lock it. I still remember his advice, and try to practice virtuous deeds, as I notice that the more you use them, the more they rub off on other people around you.

It is worth pondering upon Anger, which is described as the root cause of all other vices, as well as on love and kindness, which is the basis of virtues.

Anger

This vice torments people's lives day and night. It dwells inside every one of us. In order to keep this devil under control, we have to take certain steps.

Love and kindness are helping the world to establish strong communities. The common characteristic of both of these treasures is that the more you use them, the more you acquire and spread them. For example, if an injured person is lying and profusely bleeding on the ground, people open up their treasure of kindness and help by phoning the ambulance, calling the police, arranging for medical assistance, and so on. This practice grows every time. People have given their own lives in an attempt to save someone else. However, if people open up the wrong chest and use an element of hatred or anger, the injured person can be ignored and left to die. If one adopts an angry way of living, it keeps growing in the person until he or she is ruined.

Second, we must also be aware of the characteristics of anger inside us, and what it is capable of doing to a human being. If you read stanza (slokas) #62, and 63 in chapter two from Bhagwat Gita, you will understand that, "The man dwelling on sense-objects develops attachment from them; from attachment springs up desires, and from (unfulfilled) desire ensues anger, from anger arises infatuation; from infatuation arises confusion of memory; from confusion of memory arises loss of reason; and from loss of reason one goes to complete ruin."

The word "infatuation" is a loaded word with ugliness in every situation, which means to think ugly, speak ugly, and act ugly. This becomes a root cause of all evils. In ordinary situations, if a person gets angry, other people start saying that he looks foolish, he lacks judgment, he is infatuated, he has gone crazy, he has gone mad, he cannot think straight, he is climbing up the walls, and so on. Even a pleasing personality looks unappealing in anger.

A good person can turn bad as soon as the venom of anger overpowers him. In the Hindu religion, anger is called sin. It causes anxiety, worries, mental stress, ulcers, and all kinds of diseases in the body and mind. Anger is compared with an acid, which destroys anything you pour it on, and it destroys the vessel it is stored in.

The anger is stored inside us. A funeral pyre burns the body when it is dead, but the anger burns it while we are living. Anger comes within us when we are born. It slowly burns us while we are living. In another scripture, Ramayana's Uttar Kaand (chapter), a detailed description of anger and its effects are described, which is worth noting. Anger is the root cause of all ailments through infatuation, and from these again arise many other troubles. Lust is a counterpart of wind, and inordinate greed corresponds to an abundance of phlegm; Bile constantly burns the breast.

Should all these three combine, the result is known as *Sannipata* (a derangement of the aforesaid three humors of the body), causing a dangerous type of fever. The cravings for the manifold pleasures of the senses, so difficult to realize are the various distempers, which are too numerous to name. The feeling of ego corresponds to ringworms, envy represents itching, while joy and grief correspond to a disease of the throat marked by an excessive enlargement of its gland.

Grudging contemplation of others' happiness represents consumption; while wickedness and perversity of soul correspond to leprosy. Egoism is a counterpart of the most painful gout, while hypocrisy, deceit, arrogance, and haughtiness correspond to the disease known as *dracontiasis* (which is marked by the presence in the body of a parasite known as the guinea worm).

Thirst for enjoyment and wickedness represents the most advanced type of dropsy; while the three types of craving (those of progeny, riches, and honor at the cost of others) correspond to the violent *Quartan Ague*. Jealousy and thoughtlessness are two types of fever.

People die of one disease; while these represent many incurable diseases, which constantly torment the sou. How then can one find peace?

Third, when we know all the dangers of anger, we should take the next step for doing something about it. People meditate to quiet down the mind. Transcendental meditation is considered a very effective remedy against stress and worry, and then there are sacred vows, religious observances and practices, austere penance, spiritual wisdom, sacrifices, tapas, charity, and myriads of other remedies, which are enumerated in *Ramayana*.

One of the best activities suggested in *Bhagwat Gita* (a scripture) is to sing invocation to God, sing hymns, and hold religious gatherings. These pious activities work in a miraculous way. They cannot be analyzed, just as the bolus cannot be analyzed for what it contained. There is a matching analogy in *Ramayana* to our present context, which is fascinating and worth pondering upon. Goswami Tulsidas Ji gave a description relevant to medical terminology comparing the good and the wicked treasures. The effects of infatuation are dealt in a number of couplets –120 and 121 – in *Uttarkand*, as previously explained.

I am sure this kind of description is available in scriptures of other faiths, but I am not in a position to quote them, as I have not done any research on it. What I am writing here is simply out of my own general knowledge.

In social situations, suggestions are made to cope with the person who gets angry with you. These suggestions are worth practicing:

Acknowledge the person's anger quickly, listen closely, and never ignore or try to laugh off the anger.

Communicate with the person that you are concerned with. Typically, all the person needs is the opportunity to communicate their anger. Therefore, never try to shut the person up or hurry the person.

Keep calm. Some people express anger in an emotional way and say things they don't really mean. If you must react to their statements, do so after the problem is solved. Encourage the angry person to talk about solving the problem that caused his anger. If you listen to him calmly and show courtesy, the person's anger might go away. Talk to the person in a reasonable way and propose a specific solution to the problem.

One of the most important suggestions that people should practice is to smile a lot to cope with anger because a smile costs nothing. In fact, it spreads and gives much in return. It enriches those who receive, without making poorer those who give. It takes but a moment, but the memory of it sometimes lasts forever.

None is so rich or mighty that he can get along without it, and none is so poor but that he can be made rich by it. The smile will create happiness in the home and foster good will in business. It is the countersign of friendship. It brings rest to the weary, cheer to the discouraged, sunshine to the sad, and it is nature's best antidote to trouble. Yet it will not be bought, begged, borrowed, or stolen, for it is something that is of no value to anyone until it is given away. Some people are too tired to give you a smile. Give them one of yours, as none needs a smile so much as he who has no more to give.

The idea is that we have to try to keep our treasure chest of vices locked up, and keep our treasure chest of virtues unlocked all the time. I learned that if you get caught by a group of thugs it is extremely difficult or rather impossible to get yourself free from them unless there is a divine intervention of some sort. The five vices in your treasure chest – lust, anger, ego, greed, and attachment – are the most dangerous thugs, and once released, they will effectively execute a coordinated attack from all sides.

These thugs will not spare you by any means. If we look at the political, social, and family life in today's world, we will notice that these five thugs are tormenting us and are destroying our world. These thugs are released uncontrolled, and they are growing in leaps and bounds everywhere.

Our treasure chest of virtues, love, honesty, non-violence, humility, calmness, piety, and worship to God is always unlocked, which we can call a divine intervention. However, it is not widely used by us. There is no protection without it. This treasure chest will protect us if widely used everywhere, as it spreads uncontrolled for good to humankind.

If you think of the divine, you will be thinking of virtues. Gita tells us one thing very important that is in one couplet Lord Krishna says – you just do your duty and leave the fruit to me by surrendering to me. He further says that among all living things, the human body is high, and higher than the human body, are the senses. Higher than the senses is the mind. Higher than the mind is intellect, and higher than intellect is me.

This to me means that even a very intellectual being could execute evil deeds. However, this divine intervention of thinking of God can bring some wisdom to the intellectual being to avoid committing a bad deed like the thugs.

Environment

We hear that our life without a purpose is meaningless, just like filling water in a jug with holes in it. In our scriptures, we read that the purpose in life should be four-fold, and we need to achieve four things in life:

1. Moral righteousness, called *Dharma*;

2. Economic well being, called *Artha*;

3. Aesthetic living, called *Kama*; and

4. Spiritual liberation, called *Moksha*.

The catch is that we should achieve all four. We may find ourselves in trouble when we try to achieve only one without considering the other three.

For example, if a person keeps working without practicing moral righteousness and without enjoying aesthetic living, then it takes the usefulness of economic well-being (*Artha*). As the saying goes: "To make a living, people forget how to live."

Bhagwat Gita explains that the soul is eternal. It is neither born, nor does it die. It will not burn, and it will not sink. To realize the "Self", one must practice the four things in life to fulfill the overall purpose of life. In order to realize these four things in life, we need to talk about them, we need to practice them, and we need to experience them through our work, mind, and wealth. We need to know this through reading, listening to discourses, and going to associations of holy personalities. This is called *Saadhna* or the practice of deep concentration and meditation.

The highest purpose of *Dharma* (altruism) is to serve mankind. You might question, why should I serve mankind? The answer is that other people are no different than you. Another person is different only in body (color, race) and dress. The mind and intellect are part of a universal *Brahman* (a divine soul), which is inside us all. Therefore, when you see your divine element in others, you need to take care of others, as you take care of yourself. It is not a matter of study alone. It is a way of living.

Our environment is protected naturally if we practice the following: Harmlessness, truth, honesty, non-accumulation of wealth, purity, contentment, austerity, scriptural studies, devotion to God, spiritual wisdom, freedom from hypocrisy, straight-forwardness, absence of backbiting, spirit of humility, spirit of service, self-discipline, control of the senses, endurance, piety, forgiveness, compassion, courage, self-less meditation, freedom from malice, fearlessness, charitableness, devotion to duty, absence of egotism, and tranquility.

Today the world has advanced scientifically, technologically, and historically. The world is also experiencing the destruction of rain forests, which is reducing our supply of oxygen, medicine, exotic birds, and animals. There is excessive waste by consuming fossil fuels, which reduces the supply of renewable resources. Toxic substances currently exist in thousands of consumable and non-consumable household products in the world marketplace. Industrial pollution is reducing the supply of safe drinking water.

Today the mental, physical, and spiritual health of people is on the verge of turmoil. People's social, economic, family, and spiritual environment is not conducive to their satisfaction. We need spiritual literacy, which is most important to save our environment. We want to inculcate in us at least a minimum level of sensitivity and decency because it does not profit us to learn history or science or mathematics if we do not learn what it means to be an ethical person.

We need more and more understanding people who can bring a proper ethical perspective to their work and life. We must teach ourselves the reverence to be amazed at what a wonderful, intricate, beautiful world it is in which we live. We must learn to protect this beautiful world to allow our generations to live and enjoy. We must teach ourselves that man made technology with all its power and advancement, yet it cannot match the reverence and charisma which we enjoy from a rain fall, snow flakes, and the first flowers bursting forth in spring.

A walk in the fresh air is considered healthier than a workout on the treadmill in a closed room. Natural living through yoga and meditation is said to bring powerful results for physical, mental, and spiritual health. I may conclude by mentioning that spiritual and natural awareness needs to be placed in priority in spite of all the technological advancements in the world so that our world is environmentally sustainable for future generations.

It is so wonderful to see the technological and industrial advancement in the world today. They are making people's lives more comfortable and enjoyable. However, this comfortable and enjoyable living is only for a small segment of the world's population.

Technological advancements are not reaching billions of people around the world. The wrath of nature in the form of earthquakes, cyclones, snow, water, dust storms, typhoons, tsunamis, volcanic lava eruptions, fires, and other natural disasters at the same time is putting a mounting pressure on the lives of millions of people.

Human anger and terrorism, on the other hand, is also taking a toll on human lives without any compromise. Even the most advanced countries of the First World are unable to solve the problems of the Second and Third World countries.

We keep looking for the help of something higher than most humans' intellect and minds. I am sure we will be able to bring comfortable and enjoyable living to all human beings, as long as we keep on advancing with the help of spirituality side by side with technology.

CHAPTER FOURTEEN
Pilgrimage and Exploring India

As a retiree, once my children were married and well settled, I wanted to go touring and on a pilgrimage in India. I had two reasons to undertake a pilgrimage. One of the reasons was that I wanted to see the holy places of India, and another reason was that I wanted to see the tourist places while traveling to pilgrimage sites.

A swami once told me that if you want to see the beauty of India; want to feel the vibrations of divinity; want to enjoy the sight of fabulous monuments and awesome history; and want to experience the love of masses, then you must go on a pilgrimage in India.

A pilgrimage is a religious trip. It is a trip to visit the holy places and temples where the Lord himself resides, has manifested and set his foot in one form or the other on the face of this earth – particularly in India in this case. We call it a *Tirth Yatra* in the Hindi language. I wanted to combine this trip with visiting some historical sights and several tourist attractions, as well as taking advantage of staying at some hill stations.

My dream came true when I was charged with the responsibility of bringing divine idols from India for the temple of the Hindu Society of Manitoba. This task required me to work with the sculptor and ensure that the idols were shipped properly secured and that they reached the temple on time. I planned the trip for six months to India with sufficient time required to work with the supplier for obtaining idols in time, as well as completing my pilgrimage. This type of pilgrimage is usually undertaken together by both husband and wife.

Therefore, Kamla also accompanied me, and we both ventured on this trip from September 2005 to February2006. The work with the supplier also required conducting some meetings with local people, who were involved with the supplier, as well as communicating back and forth with the Society in Winnipeg, which I managed during the time we spent in India.

I did some research on the tourist sights, a logical sequence of visiting pilgrim places, and hill stations. I used the map of India to chalk out the route. Kamla and I finalized the plans. I coordinated all aspects of our trip including the mode of transportation, guides, board and lodging from Kashmir in the North to Kanya Kumari in the South and from Jagannath Puri in the east to Dwarika Puri in the West, along the Himalayan range, Bay of Bengal, Indian Ocean, and the Arabian sea. I also found an old book, which I used to plan each piece of our itinerary.

I noted that there are four main abodes of the Lord known as *Char Dham*, one in each direction (North, South, East and West); twelve Lord Shiva's palaces, where the Lord Shiva appeared in human form and later disappeared as a flash combined of sunlight, lamp, and fire, known as *Jyotirling*; seven holy establishments, known as *sapt puris*; palaces of triumvirate known as *Tristhali*; five holy ponds known as *punch sarovars*; fifty-two temples of the goddess of power known as *Shaktipeeth*; eighteen other important abodes; six Jain temples; seven Sikh temples; and thirteen southern *Tirthas*.

All of these Lord's abodes are situated on the mountaintops, deep valleys, vast plains, and around the riverbanks surrounded by the spectacular hill stations, historical monuments, wild safaris, and breathtaking natural beauty of India. We chose that our mode of transportation would be a van with all the comforts of a living room, a guide, and a driver. We decided that we would not drive after 7:00pm and that we would start our trip at 8:00am sharp every morning.

We first visited some of the sites in Jaipur city, before leaving for Northern India, where there are a number of hill stations and pilgrimage sites.

Hawa Mahal, the palace of winds in Jaipur city.
Jaipur is called a pink city, as its walls and home fronts are painted pink.

The crowded downtown (Johri Bazzar – left side) of Jaipur.

Same crowded market (Johri Bazzar – right side),
which is famous for gold, and jewelry shops

Public picnic park in Amber on the outskirts of Jaipur

Shisodiya Garden on the East of Jaipur

Our daughter Anita is standing by a statue circle at C-Scheme.

One of the four entrance gates of the pink city. Jaipur has four gates on its four sides, something like Quebec City in Canada.

A movie theatre for Bollywood movies
frequented by thousands every day

Kamla and family members visiting a palace in Amber

Kamla and son Dileep are resting on a hilltop.

Kamla and her friend are showing off a cannon in the
picnic grounds on a hilltop near Jaipur.

Our daughter is with her cousins at the temple grounds.

Amber Fort, north of Jaipur

Flower beds below the fort in Amber

Galta pool and temple in Jaipur

Tripolia Bazzar, a thoroughfare in Jaipur city

Kamla is plucking a flower before leaving Jaipur.

We would leave our hotel room at 8:00am after breakfast. We packed our basic items of daily necessities. We meditated upon the Lord Krishna, and with a group of our friends and relatives, we came out of our house. My mother offered her blessings. Our friends and relatives bid us farewell by offering us good wishes and by putting garlands on us. This was done according to our traditions so that no harm would come to us during our pilgrimage. We boarded our vehicle, and set out on our trip (*Yatra*) visiting Mountain Goverdhan in Gokul (a 60-kilometers area where Divine Krishna spent his childhood and youth).

I prostrated and took seven steps in the same position from the starting point to complete the *Parikrama* (circle) of the sacred mountain Goverdhan, Gokul, Mathura (birth place of Lord Krishna), Vrindavan,

Haridwar, and Hrishikesh (covering part of Saptpuri), Siriska (a tiger sanctuary), Pandupole Bharthari, and Bharatpur (a world famous bird sanctuary).

We would proceed to the cities of Haridwar and Rishikesh, which are the gateways to northern holy abodes of divine beings.

There are four places in the foothills of Himalayas. This was the second phase of our journey. We took a dip in the Holy Ganges in Haridwar at Hari Ki Pauri, which is the wide set of steps on the bank of River Ganges, and where the Indian masses take a holy bath to wash away their sins, if any. The bathers have to be very careful on the steps, as the river currents are very fast, and a slight mistake by slipping is inviting a swift sweeping away. The authorities have installed a wide metal mesh about 20 meters away to stop people who have been swept away by slipping on the steps. Kamla became a victim of the slippery steps. She had a close call. Although, she was holding a metal chain while bathing, she slipped and could not hold on to the chain. As she fell, one swimmer quickly grabbed hold of her and saved her from being sweeping away.

I am taking a dip in the Holy Ganges.

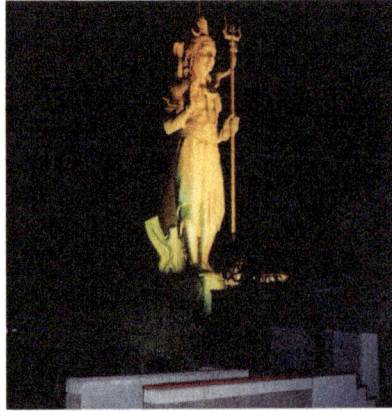

A roadside statue of divine Siva on our way to the City Rishikesh,
on the banks of river Ganges

Another beautiful roadside statue of divine Siva with his consort
Parvati, on the banks of the Holy Ganges

We took a break by the park with a statue of divine Siva with Parvati,
on the banks of the Holy Ganges on the way to Rishikesh.

Every short distance, pilgrims enjoy the beautiful sites
of roadside statues. This is also a statue of Siva and Parvati.

This is a special statue of Siva welcoming the Holy Ganges in his hair.

Rishikesh, the city of temples, on the banks of the Holy Ganges. The Swarg
Ashram (heavenly abode) is in the background. World celebrities and
pilgrims visit the Ashram for listening to revered discourses and for receiving
blessings from Swami Saraswati Muniji, who also travels to various cities in
the world. He has also visited Winnipeg several times.

Riding a gondola is one easy way to reach the temple of Mansa Devi (who fulfills your wishes) rather than walking steps straight up the hilltop.

We drove further on to the hill station Mussouri through a winding road.

Hill station roads

Mahatma Gandhi Square in downtown Massouri

A view of lush green mountain hills from the hotel balcony

Mussouri is on the way to the first temple of River Yamuna called Yamunotri at the height of 10,000 feet. It is 12 kilometers long. We rode the first 5 kilometers in a mountain jeep. You have to hike or take a palanquin carried by four porters for the remaining 7 kilometers. I decided to hike the 10,000 feet height, and Kamla decided to rent the ride of the palanquin carried by four porters. We both enjoyed our choice to reach the temple.

We arrived at the Yamunotri temple at the height of 11,000 feet.

As is the tradition, we took a dip in the hot springs before entering the temple to worship the deity Yamuna. We enjoyed the hot springs and the worship after.

I am taking a dip in the hot springs of Yamunotri.

We had only two hours to visit this temple before returning back to the base. We took some rice and flour dough to cook bread in the hot spring water for our lunch. This was a most enjoyable experience in the foothills of the Himalayas. One really finds peace in the middle of mountains and river, brooks, and trees. We returned to the base for an overnight stay.

Our next destination was Gangotri (this is where the river Ganges originates from). The Gangotri temple of the deity Ganga is situated at a height of about 11,000 feet and at a distance of 17 kilometers. There is a paved road up to the temple, and there are facilities to stay overnight for the pilgrims and tourists. We stayed overnight to enjoy the beauty of nature and to experience the spirituality at the temple. We took a dip in the cold Ganges water in the morning and arranged for a copper jug sealed with Holy Ganges water to take with us. This holy water will travel with us up to the Southern tip of India to be offered to Rameshwaram Jyotirlingam, which is situated in a splendid temple.

The origin of the river Ganges from a cave that is the shape of cow's mouth (known as Gomukh) is further at the height of another 11,000 feet and about 14 kilometers away.

A winding road on our way to Gangotri

We arrived at Gangotri temple.

The mouth of the origin of the Holy Ganges at the height of 13,000 feet and 14 kilometers north of Gangotri temple in the foothills of the Himalayas. It is called Gomukh, meaning "Cow's Mouth".

The Ganges descending in the distance by the temple

The narrow path is very treacherous and can be reached only on foot or on a horseback. A hermit lives there, and he survives on food and water casually supplied by the hikers or pilgrims. One can enjoy a close look at the Himalayas. Hikers or pilgrims need to leave Gomukh by 2:00pm every day, as there is no food or lodging overnight. One of our friends stayed with the hermit till 3:00pm in spite of the hermit's warnings. He had to walk back in darkness. At one point, he accidentally slipped and fell. He hit a tree branch and hung on to it, screaming for help. After two minutes, the branch he was hanging on to snapped, and he came crashing down to another tree.

This time the branch was a little stronger to hang on to. One pilgrim, who had already passed him, heard his screams – although almost any sound would drown in the sound of the fast-flowing river Ganges about 11,000 feet below. The pilgrim backtracked with his horse. He took about seven or eight minutes to reach the site, where my friend was hanging. Another pilgrim also joined him, who was coming right behind. The horse had a rope tied to him. The pilgrims used the rope to pull him up with great difficulty.

His wife and other friends had already arrived at the base. They checked in to their rooms, while this friend of ours had to be admitted in the hospital over night. The next morning, when his wife saw him with bruises and bandages, his ordeal came to light, and this became a widely discussed topic at the breakfast table.

The river Ganges meets river Bhagirathi, which is another name of Ganges at this confluence at Dev Prayag. This is a beautiful site to visit.

We returned to our base, Hanuman Chatti, the next day, and we rested there overnight. The next morning, we headed to another pilgrimage site, known as Kedarnath Jyotirling. We took a dip in the hot spring pool at the base and travelled to the height of about 13,000 feet and a distance of 18 kilometers. Kamla took the palanquin carried by four hired porters, and I enjoyed hiking the mountain path to the temple. The people with breathing or heart problems need to carry oxygen masks or oxygen pills with them to avoid altitude sickness. There were several medical kiosks all the way up to the mountaintop, where the temple is situated.

We, however, had a very enjoyable trip. Some people we saw went on a helicopter ride to reach the temple. There are a number of scribes on the religious resort. These scribes keep ancestry records of the pilgrims. I was surprised to see my ancestry records as far back to seven generations. I was happy to add the names of my children and grandchildren to these records. The scribes keep accurate records in the long binders and all records are handwritten. If my children ever travel there, they can add children born after my visit. The scribes get paid every year when they make house calls during winter, as the temple is closed from November to April every year due to heavy snow fall. There are no heating facilities during the winter season. This also applies to the other three temples described in this chapter.

I am hiking this single lane beaten pathway with numerous slopes on the treacherous mountain to reach Kedarnath temple, which is at a height of 14,000 feet.

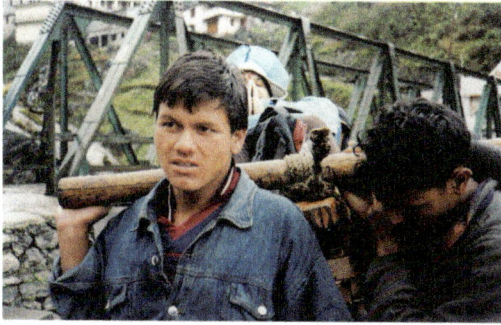

Kamla is carried by four porters, as she was encountering heavy breathing due to the height and having to use oxygen pills.

We arrived at Kedarnath temple, where we spent about four hours before having to return before darkness set in. This is a winter picture, but summer months see very little snow around the temple, although there are cool winds. The site is truly mesmerizing up in the mountains.

We returned to the base on the same day and headed to our next destination called Badrinath Temple, which is a very famous divine Vishnu's temple. There is a paved highway built by the Indian Army. The winding, snaky highway is at a height of 11,000 feet, and it is about 12 kilometers to reach the town of Badrinath. Once you enter inside the temple premise, you are immediately immersed in divine vibrations. The temple is in between two mountains and close to the border of India and China.

We drove through narrow, winding roads to Badrinath Temple. You have to be an experienced driver to pass through these roads. A slight mistake will land you in a deep gorge, costing your life. We saw a family car going down. Landslides are another danger on these roads during rainy days.

We finally arrived at Badrinath Temple, where we stayed for only three hours, as we had to drive back the same day before dark. There are motels to stay in town over night, but we decided to return.

Badrinath temple, with a beautiful background of snow-capped mountains in winter (but it is a lush green in summer)

On our return, we stopped at midway resorts to rest, enjoyed the drive, and admired the roadside statues.

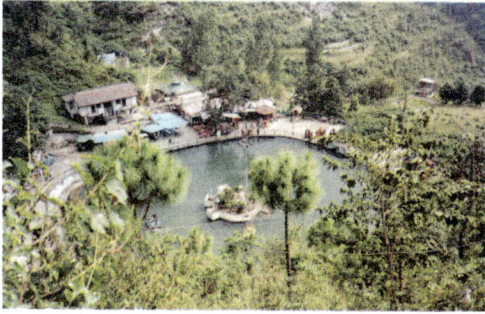

A midway resort in the hills

A close-up shot of the resort

A roadside statue of Siva

The roadside statues and midway resorts make the journey very enjoyable, as a number of restaurants, lodges, and convenience stores are attached to these places.

We greatly enjoyed these four divine abodes of Hindu Gods in the north called *Uttarakhand Yatra* (trip).

These places are covered with heavy snowfall, severe snow blizzards, piercing windstorms, avalanches, passage blockages, and extreme cold winter temperatures during the rest of the year. There is no heating system available from November to April in these ice-capped mountains, and residence facilities are closed during this period.

The snaky winding passages, water falls, deep gorges, lush green forests, and high mountain ranges are special treats for the eyes of pilgrims during May to October. Travelers come across tigers and other wild life on the winding roads near town sites. While descending towards the mainland, travelers pass through Jim Corbett's Wildlife National Park. Travelers and pilgrims throng to there by the thousands every year.

The third phase of our *Yatra* (trip) took us to Agra, the city of the Taj Mahal.

The Taj Mahal is considered the eighth Wonder of the World. It is very beautiful and very well maintained for tourists. The monument is like a dream in the shiny moonlight. We managed to shoot a bunch of good pictures of this famous monument and included ourselves in the photos.

We are enjoying our visit to the Taj Mahal.

Kamla and the Taj Mahal.

We are sitting in front of the Taj Mahal.

We also visited the cities of Fatehpur Sikri, Lucknow, Allahabad, and Sarnath on our way to Varanasi (a city of Ghats and temples of Kashi Vishvnath – one of twelve *Jyotirlings*).

We are walking towards the temple of Kashi Vishwanath, which is a famous Shiva's *Jyotirling* situated in the crowded and famous northern city of Varanasi.

This is a city that never sleeps, as there is a constant flow of pilgrims to the temples, loud chanting of hymns everywhere in the city, ongoing footsteps of yogis and swamis, and the reciting of rites by priests at the cremation Ghats.

Bodh Gaya is the main pilgrimage for Buddhist pilgrims, which is also visited by all other faiths. We kept on visiting Vaidyanath Jyotirlinga and the city of Ranchi.

Our next stop was at Bhuvneshwar (a city of 5000 temples at one time, but currently only 250 temples remained).

Maha LingRaja Siva temple

We stopped at the Konark temple, which is a very old and a very popular relic for tourists. It is a world-famous heritage site. The sun temple is situated along the Bay of Bengal on our way to Puri in O'risa state. There is a statue of the Sun God inside, and the diamond on the body glows in the dark throwing light inside.

One side wheel of the chariot of the Sun God

A public park behind us for the tourists to enjoy at Konark temple.

We drove along the shore of the Bay of Bengal, enjoying the natural beauty of vast open waters on our way to Jagannath Puri.

Soaking our feet in the Bay of Bengal.

The Jagannath Puri is one of the god's abodes in the East along the beaches and the shores of the Bay of Bengal. The god's chariot-pulling is the most important yearly festival, widely attended even by foreign tourists in Puri during the month of May.

A chariot-pulling festival in Puri

The return portion of this journey brought us to Saanchi, Bhopal, Kota, and back to Jaipur.

The fourth phase covered Sri Nath Ji temples of Nathdwara, where we rested overnight.

The next day, we visited the historical Haldi Ghati Park and museum of Maharana Pratap. The history of Maharana and his famous horse

"Chetak" is very well presented through a documentary and paintings in this museum.

The museum entrance at Haldi Ghati

Our next stop was the Akshar Dham temple of Swami Narayana at Gandhi Nagar in Gujrat State.

We had to reach Dwarka Puri (abode of divine Krishna) in the west before the sun set. Therefore, we made a short stop to visit the famous Nageshwar Jyotirling (with a 29 meters high statue of Lord Shiva next to the temple).

Nageshwar Jyotirlinga temple

A 29 meters high statue of Siva

This temple is on your way to Bhent Dwarka, where Krishna took his childhood friend Sudama and offered him riches. This place is a depiction of true friendship between a rich almighty and a poor man.

We arrived at Dwarka Puri, which is a new city, as the original Dwarika Puri in Krishna's time was submerged in the Arabian Sea, which is said to be around 42,000 years ago in Khambhat.

Having a camel ride on the sandy beach behind the temple
of Dwarka Puri, on the banks of the Arabian Sea

We saw a Shiva Lingam in the waters of the Arabian Sea.

We also visited Mahatma Gandhi's birthplace in Porbandar, where we stayed overnight and meditated in the Ashram built in his memory.

The Jyotirlinga Somnath on the shore of Arabian Sea in the west is something wonderful to see. The temple is in its glory in spite of its past history told by the locals, as it was looted of its jewels and gold 22 times, and brought to its ruins by Mohammed Gajni in past centuries. The temple inside is the same now as it was centuries ago, except the precious stones and jewels on the pillars and on its walls have been removed.

Somnath temple

We spent one night at the Gir National park of India's famous lion safari in a beautiful lodge.

A close-up shot of a lion at the park safari

We also spent another night at the Saputara lodge, where we took a Gondola ride from one mountaintop to another for daytime camping.

In front of Saputara lodge

A roadside resting place with a Shiva Lingam on the top near Saputara resort

We also visited the Junagadh's Jain temples on our way to Nasik, where the divine Rama built Panchwati to live, while in exile for 14 years. There is an interesting site where you visit Sita's bathing pond through a cave with steps. Kamla was not very careful descending through it and found herself stuck in the middle. She had to be pulled out very carefully by four men. I decided not to venture into this site.

The Jyotirling of Triyambakeshwaram, Ellora caves, Jyotirlinga Ghushmeshwaram, and Orangabaad are of great interest to tourists and pilgrims.

Visiting Ajanta caves (in the background) in Aurangabad

Jyotirlinga Ghushmeshwaram temple

Neil Mountain of Jyotirlinga Triambakeshwaram in Nasik

Ram Ghat at Nasik, a site for Kumbh Mela, where thousands
of pilgrims bathe in the holy waters

One must visit Jyotirling Bhimashankar, where you have to drive through dense jungle filled with wild animals. Later, you have to walk down about a kilometre to the temple. At the base, you need to lie down flat on your flat to behold the panoramic view of Bhimashankar River and the village from a cliff. Someone needs to hold on to both legs or you may slip into a deep gorge to never return. Travellers will never forget the awesome beauty of this place after they leave.

A roadside stop on the way to Bhimashankar Jyotirling

Bhimashankar temple

We drove through Banglore, Mysore, and Meenaxi Temple of Madurai (one must visit this ancient Parvati Temple of Lord Siva's consort), as the architectural beauty of this temple is unmatched.

Meenaxi temple in Madurai

Kanya Kumari (at the frontier and southern tip of India at a confluence of the Indian Ocean, Arabian Sea, and the Bay of Bengal) is a world-famous abode of Swami Vivekanand.

Swami Vivekanand Memorial

The Lord Shiva and his Jyotirlinga at Rameshwaram in the south along with Rama Setu was our next stop, and we stayed for two days. (Rama Setu is the bridge that Lord Rama built 7000 years ago, according to the epic story Ramayana, to cross over to what is now known as Sri Lanka to reach and finish off the demon Ravana and free his consort Sita.) Here we took a bath in the waters of the Indian Ocean and Bay of Bengal confluence. Later on, a priest poured holy waters on us from 22 different wells, as part of a ritual before we entered in the temple. The priest also poured the Ganges water we had brought from Gangotri on Lord Shiva Lingam in the temple.

We are approaching Rameshwaram, passing through a long bridge.

A thousand pillars hallway of the Rameshwaramtemple

We are taking a communal bath in the ocean before entering the temple premises. The temple is seen in the background.

A roadside statue of a demon king on our way to Tirupathi Balaji

Another roadside stop on our way to Tirupathi Balaji

We arrived at the entrance of Tirupathi Balaji temple.
We were not allowed to take any pictures beyond this point.

Along the way, we continued to Mahabalipuram, Jyotirling Mallikarjun, Hyderabad, and the Jyotirlinga Onda Nagnath.

We arrived at the Jyotirlingas Onkareshwaram and Mamleshwaram in Indore and Jyotirlinga Mahakaleshwar in Ujjain.

On the road to Onkareshwar and Mumleshwaram, with temples in the background. The word OM is also written up on the left on the hill in Sanskrit.

The temple of Maha Kaleshwaram in Ujjain. The high priest of this temple gives baths to the Jyotirlingam Maha Kaleshwaram with fresh ashes made from cow dung at 2 AM every morning. The pilgrims are allowed to watch the rituals. The ashes are collected from fresh dried cow dung cakes every day, as I was told.

We departed after an overnight stay at Ujjain to Kota, Boondi and went back to Jaipur. I also engaged in some fun activities in Jaipur like feeding a monkey and watching a show performed by snake charmers.

I am feeding the monkey.

Watching the snake charmers

This completed our *Char Dham Yatra* (four God's Abodes journey).

We enjoyed the beauty of Arabiansea in the west, Indianocean in the south, and the Bay of Bengal in the east, and their confluence at Kanya Kumari point. We relaxed at and marveled at the magnificent sights of Daruk forest, Saputara, Mt. Abu, and Kodaikanal hill stations. We took dips in Dev Sarovar (the pious water pond), the Ganges, Gomti, Narmda, Kaveri, Kshipra, and Bhimashankar Rivers. We gazed at the landscapes of the plains of Uttar Pradesh, Bihar, Madhya Pradesh,

Jharkhand, Chitorgadh, the desert of Rajasthan, and the mountain range of Himachal Pradesh and Uttaranchal.

Our fifth phase of pilgrimage, which was an addition, was to cover a 1200- kilometers journey in a sleeper coach from Jaipur to Jammu by Tavi Express train. It was an extraordinary experience on our way to Vaishnav Devi temple (where the statue of the Goddess of power, wealth, and knowledge is revered by pilgrims). Our sleeper coach also had army personnel, who were traveling to the frontier as border security. Their friendly company in the train left a permanent impression on us.

We took public bus transportation from Jammu to Katra. From Katra, we got our passes for Vaishnav Devi. I went on foot for a 12-kilometers uphill track and a 2-kilometers track on horseback, while Kamla took all of the 14-kilometers track on horseback to Vaishnav Devi temple. There is a famous stop between the town of Katra and Vaishnav Devi called Ardh Kumari. The history says that Vaishnav Devi as a teenager hid herself for nine months in 8-meters cave from a demon called Bhairav, as the demon was trying to grab hold of her with bad intentions.

The pilgrims believe that if you can crawl through the cave you get salvation from birth and death. You basically slither through this narrow cave. We waited hours in a long line to get to the entrance of the cave to begin our journey through the cave. I saw at the entrance that the opening is like a household fireplace. This created some fear inside me, although you are not supposed to have any fear in this sacred place.

I decided not to pass through the cave thinking that I was enjoying this life, and I don't mind taking birth again in the same life. So I prayed to Vaishnav Devi to excuse me for not going through it.

I got out of line with great difficulty and proceeded to meditate in the temple instead. Kamla, however, decided to go through the narrow cave and succeeded without any difficulty. It is said that even the most obese person has no difficulty passing through this cave. You just keep slithering forward, keeping your eyes focused on the lighted picture of the Devi, and at the end of the tunnel, you are simply pulled up by three or four men to the upper platform. I will, however, not recommend this slithering through the tight cave to any one who is claustrophobic because you are inside a mountain.

It was snowing heavily when we went up there in the first week of February. We had to stand in line for two hours, barefoot in the cold snow-filled pathway, while it was snowing. We got a glimpse of Vaishnav Devi only for 30 seconds when we reached the throne in the temple. The deity is known and worshipped for ultimate powers of Energy, Wisdom, and Wealth, and can be seen only in three stone-shaped figures known as *Pindis*.

Kamla and I are riding horseback on our way to the Vaishnav Devi temple.

We arrived at the temple of Vaishnav Devi, which is situated on top of the Trikoot mountain. It is covered in snow, as we went in February. It was cold. We stayed overnight at the motel next to the temple.

It is said that you should not be looking at the beautiful pictures placed above the Pindis, as you are warned ahead of time to look at the Pindis only. Vaishnav Devi swiftly whirled as a wind from the tunnel after hiding for nine months. She destroyed the demon Bhairav by chopping off its head and established herself in the form of three Pindis on the throne. Demon Bairav's head fell off a few kilometers away. After realizing his mistake, he pleaded for mercy, which was granted to him as compassion triumphed over the rage.

The pilgrims also visit Bhairav's temple on their way out. After standing in the snow for almost three hours, I thought to myself that I might catch a cold. However, I slept like a baby in warm blankets in the hotel overnight, and I was in perfect health in the morning. This was the most memorable *yatra* (trip) for us.

We returned to Jammu in the State of Jammu and Kashmir and stayed overnight to visit "The Raghunath" temple, which houses the mini idols of 33 million gods. The temple entrances were heavily guarded at that time because it was a target of militant terrorists a few years ago.

We were able to roam around freely the next day in Jammu's famous "Baghe Bahu" public park on the banks of Tavi River.

I took a walk in Baghe Bahu park in Jammu.

We were getting close to our time of returning back to Canada with the temple idols, and we left India in the second week of February. We covered the entire peninsula of India by driving about 23,000 kilometers in four phases of three and half months.

We enjoyed our driving trip because of our skilled driver. We consumed bottled water worth over 6000 rupees during our trip. We spent over 5000 rupees as a payment to the local priests (called *pandas*) at each temple we visited for their deserving service that took us closer to the deities in the temples. We had to spend close to 4000 rupees to pay for some extortion to local *gundaas* (Hindi word for hoodlums) in various cities and highways where our car was stopped at gunpoint just for the sake of making easy money. We learned that kind of extortion was quite common at a number of places we visited. We also had to spend a few thousand rupees to pay bribery to the policemen at the border crossings at each state due to their corrupt system.

This was the negative experience we had to go through which was not very significant compared to the positive experience of visiting the extraordinary sights of the splendid and magnificent temples and hill stations. We enjoyed our hotel stay and meals because of our travel guide. We enjoyed our vantage point for viewing the deities in every temple because of the hiring of local priests.

We learned that the love, friendship, and communion of thousands of pilgrims, devotees, and tourists, are always there during the *Yatra* (spiritual journey) when you mingle with the people. We learned that in order to complete your spiritual journey (*Tirth Yatra*), first you need to pick up a copper bangle from Jagannath Puri, and then you offer this bangle to Badrinath deity. You pick up Holy Ganges water from Gangotri (the origin of the holy river Ganges), and then you take this holy water to the Lord's abode in Rameshwaram and offer it to Lord Rameshwaram.

You pick up the holy soil of the Rameshwaram from the Indian Ocean after bathing in it and offer it to Triveni Sangam (the confluence of three rivers – Ganges, Yamuna, and Saraswati) at Allahabad. Finally you go to Pushkar, a place of fifty ponds and the only temple in the world of Lord Brahma, the creator, and take a dip in the *Brahma Kund* (holy pond). This completes the spiritual journey.

We completed the spiritual part of our journey. We left the historical landmarks unattended due to the lack of time at our disposal, and we plan to visit some other time. The journey we completed was a memorable one, which we will never forget as it has touched our hearts forever.

We saw piles of garbage thrown by people around the temples and pathways. The people living in the towns and cities do not put garbage in one place to be collected but throw it wherever they please. Even the pilgrims leave plastic water bottles, garlands, flowers, coconut shells, unused dirty containers, broken glass bottles, dirty garments, and all sorts of filth while traveling. People use the bathroom on the open ground and leave kilos of human waste everywhere. The open bathrooms are never cleaned or sanitized for the users. Before closing the temple, the temple priests and workers push tons of leftover offering ingredients behind the temple premises, after the worship of the deities is performed. The sweepers come to clean the places during the busy time of day, when hundreds and thousands of people are around.

We ate piping hot meals at every stop to keep ourselves healthy. We always avoided ice cubes, ice cream, and cold salad at the roadside restaurants at our doctor's advice. Our hotel room every day was very clean at a reasonable rate between 600 to 800 rupees per night with double occupancy. Our total cost of this journey was about 250,000 Indian rupees, which was the equivalent of about $7000 Canadian. At the end of our journey, we found that we were very rich in our travel experiences, and also that we had collected hundreds of booklets and video CDs of each place we visited. We now enjoy watching these CDs, looking at the pictures we photographed, and reading the stories about each place we visited.

I successfully brought all the idols for the temple, which was under construction, and about to be completed in June 2006. The idols and altars safely arrived in the containers in April, which I shipped from Jaipur city on February 12, 2006. We also left for Canada on the same day.

The Society scheduled the deities to be installed in June 2006, and the Society was kind enough to assign me the responsibility for the installation and with the ceremony of life instilling in the deities in the altars. Hindus believe that life needs to be instilled in stone deities through religious rituals and mantras before starting to worship them in the temples. The mason who carved the deity's statues also built the altars. He came to Winnipeg for the purpose of fixing the proper altar. The Society was also kind enough to recognize me by awarding a plaque during a public gathering in recognition of my volunteer work as the President of the Society.

The plaque was presented to me by the Hindu Society of Manitoba in a public ceremony for my voluntary work as President of the Society.

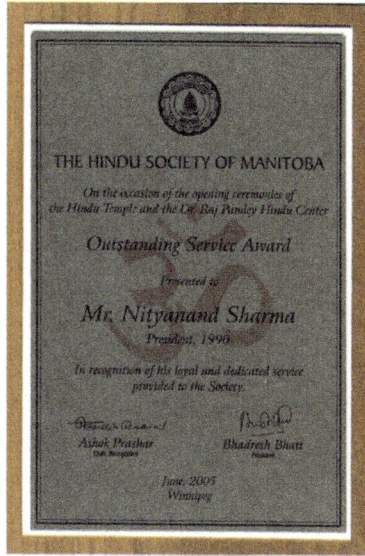

The plaque

CHAPTER FIFTEEN
Retirement

I am still devoting my volunteer time to the Hindu Society of Manitoba. First, I was elected as Chairman of the Temple in 2007 for a term of two years, and then I was elected to the Board of Trustees for a term of four years. In 2011-12, I was serving as the Chairman of the Board of Trustees.

In March 2012, I suddenly felt a pain in my chest, while working in the backyard garden. I phoned the medical centre to seek advice about if I had anything serious that I should be concerned about. Based on the description of my pain, the nurse in-charge suggested that I was having a heart attack. She told me instead of wasting time in talking to her, I should call an ambulance immediately, which I did. I was admitted in the hospital for a quick EKG, and I was diagnosed that my three arteries were blocked – one 97%, and other two 87%. I was quickly hauled to the Cardiology ward and fitted with two metal stents in the main artery that was 97% blocked.

After a night's rest in the hospital, the attending physician and cardiologist asked me if I wish to have by-pass heart surgery or more stents in the other two arteries that were 87% blocked. They said that putting stents in is a good option, if a patient does not wish to go through with heart surgery. After conversing with my family and friends, I decided that more stents would be a good option. The cardiologist fitted me with four more drug eluting stents, two in each artery. I was thoroughly counseled by the team of doctors, the cardiologist, and the pharmacist to follow up with regular exercise, medication, stress-free life routines, and a disciplined diet in order to stay healthy for the rest of my life. I decided that now was the time to fully retire from any work except to follow what was advised.

I joined the re-fit centre, where I was thoroughly checked, and put in to a regulated exercise regime, which I continued, even after leaving the re-fit center. Currently, I am maintaining my healthy lifestyle.

Every day, I do the treadmill for 30 minutes, the stationary bike for 7 minutes at a prescribed speed, yoga for 15 minutes, stretch & strength exercises for 10 minutes, and meditation for 15 minutes. I follow this daily routine religiously. I monitor my medication regime and eat a healthy diet of vegetables and fruits according to my doctor's advice. I try to stay away from situations that may cause stress. I feel happy and healthy at 76 years of age.

Kamla is also very supportive and regularly helps me maintain my schedules on a daily basis. She tells me that I have to follow the doctor's prescriptions, and that I have to treat the prescribed medicines like offerings. She also takes her medication for thyroid, blood pressure, and cholesterol, but she does not do exercise with me, as she has joined the city pool and takes swimming classes to get her exercise.

Before, the heart attack, I used to drive to Calgary for 14 hours straight, but now I need to stay overnight, as I cannot bear the stress of continuous driving. I also avoid extreme cold and hot temperatures during the day or night. My healthy routines have helped me maintain a healthy body free from any complications so far.

Currently, I am downsizing, and I want to keep my computer work at a minimum, so that I am moving more than sitting in one place. At one point, I even decided to disconnect my Internet service just to get away from too much reading. I informed my family of my intentions through a poem by e-mail, which became a laughing matter among them saying that I would never be able to maintain this decision. I wrote to them as follows:

Poem 8

As soon you step outside your home, there is, everywhere, free Wi-Fi;

For operating our devices, on Hotspots, we generally keep an eye.

For information, easy access, & excessive material, at this time;

Phone choices i.e. Vonage, net-talk, magic jack, com-wave, & land line.

TV choices i.e. netFlix, Shomi, Crave TV, Neo-TV, apple-TV, & Jadoo-TV;

Free Range TV, mobile TV of all sorts, but nothing like cable TV.

E-mails, Skype, Face time, Google Hangout, & online communication;

Photo share, i-cloud storing, online shopping, can be a big confusion.

Online banking, e-bills, e-notifications, e-donations, do I need this time;

All I need is live cable TV and Hollywood movies and a land phone line.

We will miss the choice of Face time or Hangout, anytime with you all;

But this can be arranged from Pinky's home or from Wi-Fi in a mall.

You all have smart phones to contact us at your own convenience;

I can check emails several times at the library/mall at my convenience.

I can skip Facebook, YouTube, Web-MD daily, until later;

Excessive material too much to digest, soon can be retrieved anywhere.

Utility bills, taxes, medical premiums, and groceries are constantly on rise;

Inability to raise income at this age, a pension remains to manage life.

Austerity measures, and downsizing is a wise step to take for a pensioner;

Temporary suspension of Net is not much to loose from May to October.

I have not seen or listened to my good collection of DVDs and cassettes;

"Oh! Life was so much easier twenty years ago" without Internet.

I now truly feel like a retired person. I look at my plaque that was presented to me by INAC.

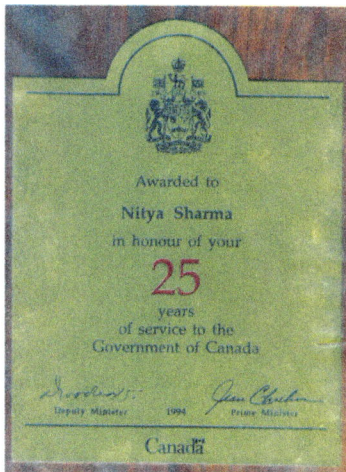

Awarded to

Nitya Sharma

in honour of your

25

years
of service to the
Government of Canada

Deputy Minister   1994   Prime Minister

Canada

This is the plaque for my loyal service to the Government of Canada.

I also look at my picture with an umbrella-like turban put on me by my relatives, recognizing me as the head of my family after my father's death in India.

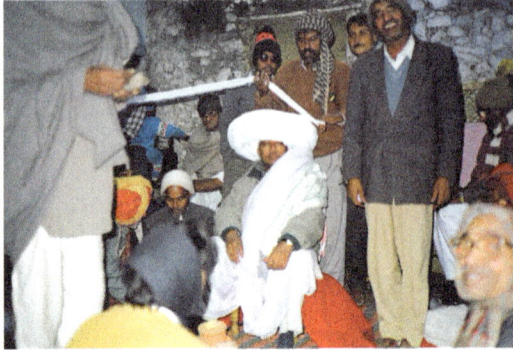

My relatives are decorating me with a turban with offerings
by the relatives to recognize me as the head of the family.

Writing my memoirs is something that keeps me occupied in remembering my life's activities. I am sure, readers will also enjoy reading my autobiography and seeing the beautiful pictures of landmarks we visited in India and Canada.

Both Kamla and I are relaxing after our trips in
Canada and pilgrimage trips in India.

CHAPTER SIXTEEN
Reminiscing

Kamla and I reminisce over coffee every morning. We talk about our life in India, and now in Canada. We remember the time Kamla spent in my absence for three years with both girls, while I was teaching in Canada. I remember to tell her how I prepared the household after sponsoring them to Canada. We talk about the special youth workshop on Hinduism and rituals, including a gala community dinner, which was initiated by me in a Board of Directors' meeting in March 1991 when I was the President of the Hindu Society of Manitoba as a volunteer.

We talk about the leadership role I demonstrated during my work life with the Government of Canada at the Department of Indian and Northern Affairs Canada. We talk about Kamla's contribution of looking after the family in Canada, including our children's education, marriage, and overall family health. We talk about Kamla's contribution to the Society as a volunteer and the recognition letter she received from the President. We talk about our children's progressive lives they are leading with their families. We talk about living only in Winnipeg, Manitoba, as we love Winnipeg and our life in Winnipeg. We love Canada.

CPSIA information can be obtained
at www.ICGtesting.com
Printed in the USA
LVOW05*0710180717

541677LV00015B/145/P

9 781525 506536